PARITY DEMOCRACY

How to Level the World Economic Playing Field

Written

By

Ed Wode

Published in USA by
Horned Toad Productions, Inc.
Long Beach, Ca. 90810
Distributed by lulu.com and HTP, Inc.
License type: Creative Commons Attribution-
Non Commercial Share Alike 2.0
ISBN: 978-0-6151-3856-5
This is a progressive book.

TABLE OF CONTENTS

PARITY DEMOCRACY

PARITY DEMOCRACY

How to level the world economic playing field!

"I only presume to offer hints"
Tom Paine

"I give you a republic, but can you keep it!"
Benjamin Franklin

Chapter 1.

American Democracy, the Political Problem

Unfortunately, nothing could be more naive than to think that an honest or even alert citizenry can deal with the complex ambiguity of American government; at least not well enough to protect what is in fact an amoral code that at best provides for an unenlightened liberty, no matter how vigilant is any, individual. Once reforms have been made, as they have been many times in this country, abuses not only creep back, they leap back. This is because not only are the principles of democracy in America abused and not observed, but they are ill conceived to start with. Discovering the nature of true democracy is one of the missions of this book. Identifying the basic political problem of democracy in America is the mission of this chapter.

American representative democracy, it has been claimed, started with the ideas of Tom Paine. Tom Paine saw man as a social animal, which, out of the necessity of his environment, was forced to enter into cooperative activities. According to Paine, man in the state of nature is possessed of liberty and equality. He entered into government because the need for human cooperative activity made unregulated existence intolerable. Government, therefore, was created as a regulator of the social contract between equals, as opposed to something imposed on the weaker by the stronger. It seems then, from this argument, that the key element of democracy should be the protection of the weaker from the predatory nature of the stronger. This protection is necessary to make cooperative activity profitable enough for everyone to create an order based on some form of equality. There is no distinction as to whether predators are kings, criminals, dictators, monopolists or pedants; the weaker must be protected from the stronger. Even when the stronger is a majority voted into power by free elections, the weak must be protected by government's recognition of various inalienable rights of man. Paine favored enumerated rights, such as those in the Bill of Rights, to protect man's inalienable natural rights.

The American constitution has the additional protection of checks and balances that are also designed to prevent absolute majority rule. Paine did not favor checks and balances, as he found their complexity made them ineffectual in the British constitution to keep the monarch from becoming a despot. Right here is the crux of the American political problem: throughout our history we have failed to adequately protect the rights of minorities. At one time or another we are all part of a minority in America; thus, we have all been suffering in varying degrees because we have no real understanding of what our individual rights are and, therefore, no way to mandate these rights. We will continue to suffer uncertainty and face chaotic conditions until we clearly enumerate the most essential individual rights. First, however, we must understand what these rights are. If we face this challenge, we will, for the first time in our history, have the possibility of a government based on a definite unambiguous moral compass. For the first time we will also have a government immutably dedicated to the welfare of all the people, instead of some of the people. We will also have the beginnings of a continuity that will mean that whoever is elected President of the United States will be required to uphold the laws and keep his or her promises or be removed forthwith from office. No intervening authority, such as congress or the Supreme Court, should be able to prevent this removal in case it is needed to punish malfeasance. If we cannot do this, we are vulnerable to the possibility of electing a dictator.

In the Constitution, Paine's protection of minority rights was converted from the specific protection of individual rights to the general protection of checks and balances. Unfortunately, this conversion of principles provides the main reason democracy has not flowered properly in America: because of slavery and other prejudicial practices, the Founding Fathers were unwilling from the first to face up to the main element of protection of individual rights - minority rights. And this seed of despotism has allowed the formation of a new aristocracy in America; the aristocracy of money that, for the most part, has been dominant ever since.

Because of this dominance of predators, we have had many mini-revolutions known as reform movements. They have been non-violent, for the most part, and have been at times instrumental in bringing about good reforms and a higher degree of democracy, sometimes permanent. But, alas, all our efforts have been to fight the symptoms of the disease instead of the primary cause stated above. The disease has always returned, and always will return, until we cure it once and for all. If the rights of minorities were truly protected, the character of American democracy would be entirely different from what it is. People would be able to "do their own thing" and live according to their own choice of lifestyle without becoming outcasts or outlaws. We might not have fifty million single people who prefer to live lonely lives rather than take on the responsibility of family, because of the financial pressures of contemporary American life.

Family life in America has been destroyed by economic pressure. It is simply much easier to let someone else take the responsibility for the next generation. Americans have been cheated out of their birthright without even realizing it. We are all victims of the great illusion that we are rich because we live in America. Rich in what? People in poor third world countries are able to have large families. Many Americans cannot afford even one child without courting bankruptcy. This is because a new mouth to feed requires an expensive change in their lifestyles to accommodate children - by buying a home, for example. Almost no one in America can afford to buy a house anymore, unless they are willing to risk gambling on a very risky financial bubble.

Finally, if individual rights were truly protected, everyone would be constitutionally guaranteed a job, health care, a free genuine education, as opposed to the free pseudo education we now receive and other things necessary to make men free and equal; the most important of which is security. Security for the forgotten man was Roosevelt's main objective with the New Deal. Now, after trying for over 60 years to give our citizens security, we have hardly what could be called pseudo security. Everything in this country seems to be pseudo, so why not pseudo-security? A democracy of bottom line security is the democracy that has been denied us by the Founding Fathers. They gave us, not democracy, but pseudo democracy.

The fight for these things called individual rights is the story of democracy in America. With the advent of the Bush 2 administration, after more than two hundred years of struggle, Americans are further from the realization of these essential rights than they have ever been before. The reason is that George W.Bush and his cohorts of the Republican Party pretend to stand for individualism but really stand, not for individual rights, but for the right of corporations and other business concerns to do as they please with the American system. And the people have little or no protection against these predators, if their representatives in congress and the President are biased against them. This is because, while political checks and balances were built into the Constitution, they have little or nothing to do with individual rights. The main body of the Constitution is about protecting political freedom. The right to vote. The right of majority rule. But, as I have said, it was recognized by Tom Paine and others that the majority is not always right. I am convinced in fact that the majority is very often wrong. This is a great weakness of the democratic system. Not because the majority is composed entirely of stupid people, but because often it has trusted leaders who have deceived everyone by hiding their own true agenda. This is why the Constitution was originally amended. The Bill of Rights, or the first ten amendments to the Constitution, was an attempt to recognize that certain individual rights must be guaranteed because the simple political freedom of the Constitution on paper is not enough to bring about actual freedom and equality. It is a thesis of this book that these guarantees, while important in and of themselves, have not been enough to allow democracy to fully bloom in America.

What we need to do is pick up where President Roosevelt intended his "New Deal for the forgotten man" to blossom before his untimely death. We have made little or no progress toward FDR's Economic Bill of Rights that should have been considered with the greatest seriousness, as it has never been. The Supreme Court and the Congress have truncated other aspects of his program and substituted a body of laws that are full of loopholes and favoritism for special interests. That means we must amend the American Constitution to guarantee real security for every human being in this country. Otherwise we will make the same mistake reforming liberal leaders since Roosevelt have made; that of trying to fight a forest fire with a water pistol. But are such amendments possible without a real revolution? At this point, probably not, unless we can wrangle a new constitutional convention. Newt Gingrich's phony-baloney right wing revolution was successful in continuing the democracy myth, not the real thing. It was preeminently successful in helping make America a country of the dumb by the dumb for the dumb.

It remains to be seen whether America survives this dumb revolution. Many of our finest young people have been sacrificed so that this dumb bunch can bully the world into serving their interests. The interests of corporate America. Unless there becomes a calamitous necessity for revolutionary ideas, as I think is entirely possible considering the stupid dishonest group now in charge, a peaceful left of center revolution will not accomplish much. People are too damn dumbed down by lying pundits in the media and government to know what is in their own best interest. The mission of this book is to put in place a blueprint of democratic ideas for real democracy as opposed to the pseudo version we now have so that they will be there at a time when they may be desperately needed.

In 1929 the American brand of democracy virtually collapsed. That was one year after Calvin Coolidge, a hero to former President Reagan, left office at the height of American prosperity. The country was being led by a new president Herbert Hoover, who had had no time to change the system in any significant way from how fellow Republicans had been running it and how he intended to run it. Hoover's policies were the same as those of Coolidge until after the crash when the country, as if by cardiac arrest, just collapsed economically. At the end of his term

Hoover ran for reelection committed, with his fellow Republicans, to the same policies that had resulted in collapse.

Institutions and stooges of the Republican Party never die, they just creep back like rattlesnakes with renewed doses of poison. According to the June 3, 1981 L.A. Times the Moral Majority's Nelson Bunker Hunt and William B. Bright, head of the Campus Crusade for Christ, were among financial leaders at a Financial Success Seminar headed by William C. Wagner where there were repeated calls for a return to the gold standard (So this is who the Moral Majority really was). They are now back, as the born again neoconservatives, stronger than ever and in full control of the country. They have new masters, however, the transnational corporations. In line with the policies of these multi national new masters, they have dismantled their former high tariff mantra (Intended to protect their domestic U.S. business patrons) in favor of the mantra of their new masters, the free global traders. It is however only free for the corporations to downgrade and outsource American worker's jobs and disregard any semblance of responsibility for worker security, even obligations already incurred such as pensions. This is a very expensive revolution for American workers. It is clear that even if the road map has changed to an unrecognizable

Republican agenda, we are headed to the same destination for almost the same reason that took us to collapse in the 1930's. In some ways and for some people we have already reached that destination. Unfortunately, we have never been sure why these freebooting Republican policies of former times caused collapse, or we would probably not risk taking the same road again. Prosperity, or pseudo-prosperity, has cooled our wrath to the point where what was clear to us in the 1930's is not so obvious today. "The forgotten man", or out of deference to women what should today be called the little people who are being ignored, is the main problem. The ignored little people were then and are now, in deep trouble. If a large body of people are in trouble there is obviously going to be big trouble at some point.

Franklin Roosevelt ran against Hoover in 1932 on a Democratic platform that promised the country all of the advantages of the Republicans - plus a great deal more. It attacked the Republican high tariff and promised a tariff for revenue in its place. In addition, they promised a program of economic and social reform that would improve things for everyone. They promised domestic and foreign renewal. The Republicans, on the contrary, blamed our problems on foreign causes. Roosevelt mainly attacked our domestic weaknesses instead. He stressed the plight of the average citizen, claiming that our economic system under the Republicans guaranteed security for only a small part of the population. He convinced the country that if the Democrats were elected, the average citizen - the forgotten man - would receive a new deal.

This new deal has never been allowed to come to full fruition. Instead, we find ourselves, in spite of many improvements started by Roosevelt, back to where the system is becoming, or has become, terribly difficult for the average or small person. Housing is becoming prohibitively expensive, high paying factory jobs are scarce and disappearing fast, prices are high and interest rates are rising again. In other words, we have gotten much of the old deal back in a slightly different scenario. Anyone who is not at all times employed in a well paying job is quickly sentenced to poverty. It is quite clear that this situation under Bush 2's management of government is going to worsen by the day, since it is the obvious, if not stated, policy of that government to do the least for the most. "We are going to get a chance to spend our money, instead of the government spending it for us" say these masters of deceit. When inflation comes back and prices go up, let us see how much more we have to spend. The three

G's will have all the money, God, Gates and Google - at least one out of three is not evil.

Playing the prophet of doom doesn't suit me, as I am a very positive person and believe in positivism. I just believe we are making a mistake trying to turn the clock back, and will eventually have to pay a heavy price for it. If the worst occurs, we should have some contingency plan. Bush's ideas as hitherto expressed don't offer a clue for economic salvation. It is a plan for status quo. He claims, according to his State of the Union address 06, to be aware of our need to improve our competitiveness. But where is the plan to do so? His deeds never match his rhetoric. Everything, everything depends on our regaining our competitive edge. This is an absolute necessity unless the world economic order is changed, as it should be. As it will be, if the ideas in this book are put into play. Unfortunately Republicans don't believe in plans. The Iraq war best illustrates this. I look toward the future and see the possibility of a different world, an exciting world based on a lot of action. First and foremost: economic action that empowers American entrepreneurs to be able to compete on a level playing field in any industry with anyone in the world. That is why I consider this book a twenty-first century futurist economic-political philosophy. This is an alternative plan to economically democratize the entire world. It is a backup plan in case the present world economy becomes such a disaster that a wide consensus of people demands change. In my opinion, the present way of globalizing the world economy already is a total disaster.

How has the cycle returned to inaction after what we went through in the thirties? Prosperity has mellowed the edge of resentment and, we might add, dulled the memory of its justifiable outrage. The fiends of greed, and the rest of us who just like to make a lot of money, never cease moneymaking efforts that, after a lapse of enough time, results in the impoverishment of the rest of the human race. The rest of the human race being those who are not successful enough in the game of economic musical chairs to come to roost on the money chairs.

Even before Roosevelt completed his program of economic revival, which did revive the business cycle (Previously totaled) and restore the people's confidence in the viability of the American system, it was attacked, inhibited by obstruction and to some degree, dismantled by the Supreme Court. An amazing amount of new programs and reforms were begun that revolutionized the American system in spite of the problems encountered. It is clear that without these reforms and the ensuing economic recovery we would have been prostrate in the face

of World War II. The war spurred an already recovering economy into

full recovery and full employment. That Roosevelt saved the capitalist

system in this country by instituting socialist type reforms is beyond a

question of a doubt, except in the eyes of those who benefited most by

this recovery, the masters of greed and their running dogs.

Soon after their promulgation many key New Deal laws were

declared unconstitutional by the Supreme Court of the United States,

usually by narrow margins of 5 to 4. The Court then was mostly

composed of holdover conservatives from the Republican

administrations preceding Roosevelt. These high court decisions

stopped in its tracks the democratic revolution started by Roosevelt.

At the time, many people wanted constitutional amendments

preventing the court from dictating to the country the limits of

democracy. That is what these majority conservatives on the Supreme

Court did. We now know this would have been the correct course of

action. However, Roosevelt, impatient to get the job done in a hurry,

opted for other tactics. Tactics that unfortunately were not effective.

We may soon have to face up to the fact that the only way to have

democracy in this country is to learn from the Roosevelt experience, especially the two most important lessons outlined above: the small people must have a fair deal if there is to be permanent prosperity and we are going to have to amend the constitution, extending individual rights, if we are to achieve permanent prosperous real democracy. Our present system allows the villains, by their greed and heartlessness, to usurp the right of everyman to a fair deal. We must find a way to end the living pressure cooker that has become the American system and find a way to have inexpensive housing, low prices, low interest, plentiful jobs and security for everyone. And if we are to have these things, the government is going to have to spend a lot of our money and energy, the right way for a change. And of course, we must have people in government who stand for these things and not just for the bottom line of global corporations.

Now, we have created a mentally ill society that is tottering closer every day to the brink of self-destruction, arms madness, and total chaos. How is it that the American system seems to always gravitate toward self-destruction? (The last depression was not our first) A clique of men known as the Federalists ruled America, from the time of its inception until the time of Thomas Jefferson's election in 1800. Most of these men had little confidence in the ability of the little people to govern themselves. These men believed that only the merchants, the financiers, the large landowners, and the educated men knew what was best for the country. In what one could call the first peaceful revolution, "the unlawful insurgents (rebels), anarchists and rabble", as they were called by the Federalists, banded together, formed a political party and elected a President, Jefferson. Thus began, in America, the battle of the haves against the have-nots that has characterized American politics ever since. This battle has taken many shapes and forms and many names, sometimes with groups, which were formerly opponents realigning themselves into new confederacies as their interests changed. Upward mobility came with peaceful political revolutions, transforming have-nots into haves and radical into conservative. Consistently, whenever a group has been successful politically, that group has put its own special interests ahead of the interests of the country as a whole. Fortunately, these peaceful revolutions usually have resulted in reforms that have been good for all parties. The result of all this strife has been a procrustean system that has torn at itself to the point where we have no predictable continuity of government in America. It does seem to be a law, however, that America periodically needs an attempt to reform the system.

In spite of all constitutional guarantees and amendments, the changeover of one party to another has often radically altered the balance of power between those who stand for the preeminence of unchecked individual and/or corporate power and those who purport to represent a more democratic and equal distribution of wealth. Jefferson was brought to power to check the abuses of the Federalists and improve the conditions of the people. Jefferson did radically change the course of American government and satisfy the limited needs of his constituency. After Jefferson, the country went through a period of rapid development that provided plenty for everyman. Then the industrial revolution in the Northeast placed the interests of powerful industrialists in conflict with the needs of the workingman, who usually preferred to be a farmer and work for himself. The manufacturers of the Northeast did everything in their power to have the government pass laws restricting the sale of cheap Western lands to the people in order to keep cheap labor plentiful for their factories. The common man again revolted and the Democratic Party was brought to power for the first time with Andrew Jackson at its head.

Jackson promoted the national welfare of the country over sectional interests, which best fulfilled the needs of his constituency. Western lands were made available more cheaply than ever to the common man and this resulted in a rapidly developing America. For the first time in our history federal funds were used by Jackson for local improvements and the welfare of the common man. But the victory of the little people was, as usual, short lived. After Jackson left office in 1857 the sectionalists and special interest groups ran the country according to their whims until their excesses prompted the reform movement of Teddy Roosevelt in 1901.

Recognizing the excesses and evils of our economic and political life, T. Roosevelt outdid all his predecessors in restraining Big business. He was known as the great trustbuster, although his successor Taft did more trust busting than he did. However, many of the reform acts we cherish today came about under T. Roosevelt. Interestingly, there was a great debate during these times as to whether corporations should be allowed at all. The great trusts and monopolies, some of which were broken up, had instilled great fear in political leadership because of their great economic power. Serious consideration was given to prohibiting the corporate form altogether.

It was decided that as long as the government was strong enough to control them it had nothing to fear from corporations. The corporations it was decided had a role to play in the American economy, as long as they played by the rules. Therein has become our dilemma. Not only don't they play by the rules, corporations now make the rules. Unfortunately, many political leaders soon forgot this debate and this fear and have throw in their lot with the corporations. Corporate power is now such that they are more powerful than any government on earth and as such are buying and selling governments at will. Our American government is no exception. We are in fact a de facto corporate dictatorship. This is why for years you have heard the corporate sponsored mantra that big government is bad. What is really meant by this is that big government is bad for corporations and weak government is good. Only a very powerful people controlled government can protect us from the depredations of corporations. The opposite is the case. The tail is now wagging the dog.

After World War I, as a result of the greatly expanded industrial base and the reforms of the Wilson administration, there was great prosperity in America under Republicans Harding, Coolidge and the first year of ill-fated Herbert Hoover. These presidents did very little to reform anything. Part of the charming Republican syndrome I call anarchism, which goes back to the Federalist idea that the least government is the best government, is that they don't change much, at least for the better. Government, of course, is the only power that can effectively control, the excesses perpetrated by corporate lobbyists that the Republicans have come to represent. This is why they claim big government is bad. The Republican Party is really the Federalist establishment that has been with us since the beginning (Having only changed its name to suit the times) that thinks nothing needs to be done while in office except roll back the democratizing work of other parties, cut taxes for the rich and in modern times feed the military/industrial complex.

Of course until the cold war there was no military/industrial complex. The Republican favored high tariff policy, in place until the advent of the multi-national corporation, was largely responsible for turning the business cycle downward, with its final culmination being the crash of '29 and the beginning of the long period of total economic collapse known as the Great Depression. Of one thing I am certain: The "crash" was the cumulative effect of the policies of the Republican Party that ignored the needs of the little man while they pandered to their sponsor's big business. Hoover, after one year in office, when nothing had time to drastically change, cannot be charged with full responsibility for the depression. Only the uninformed would come to such a conclusion. A faulty system that allows the predators to kill the goose that lays the golden egg was the culprit then and is the culprit now that is allowing the dismantling of the American system. We the geese are now being plucked of our jobs, our security, and our constitutional rights while the conglomerate owned media stuffs our heads with a lot of mindless distractions that mask our corporate caused problems and sets us up for another great fall. The military-industrial-government establishment has not only fleeced us, as feared by Eisenhower, but we have had our government completely gobbled up by the transnational corporations. Only the stupid no longer silent majority don't realize we are now a government of the corporations, for the corporations by our legislative bribe takers who under the Republicans only represent corporate interests. Let us hope this changes with the new Democrat congress, but the seeds of K street corruption are already in place ready with their filthy lucre to seduce the susceptible. Unfortunately, it is we the geese who always end up with the worst case of indigestion. It may soon be lethal pandemic. Our only consolation is that the mistakes of the fathers can be biblically passed to the next generation. Who says all those creationist ideas in the bible aren't evolutionary?

This has been a real nutshell encapsulation of American political-economic history intended to impress upon the reader that our present problems are not new, contrary to uninformed belief. The struggle for everyman's fair share of the democratic pie has been going on since the founding of the republic. It has often been a knock-down-drag-out fight between the haves and the have-nots. This struggle will continue to tear at the fabric of this republic until we are successful in creating true democracy. It is the belief of this writer that if we do not solve this problem of whether to have or not to have democracy once and for all, we are not going to be able to solve the major problems that now face this nation. Placing a disproportionate amount of our national budget into arms production and unnecessary wars is highly detrimental and very "unbalanced", to use Ike's terminology, to every peacetime program. It is always easiest to wave the flag when it puts bucks in your pocket. If we do not solve our other national problems, that are all basically problems of whether to have or not to have democracy, we are sure to once again go bust; and this time we will risk being completely discredited in the eyes of the rest of the world. It is highly recommended that every adult American familiarize himself with the main props of the American system of democracy. Only then can you truly hope to be intellectually qualified to go to the polls and choose a proper leader.

American history speaks loudly for itself. The more prosperous the people become because of equalizing reforms, the more prosperous is the nation as a whole. The more democracy is undermined by the despots of greed, sectional interests and one-sided policies that favor big money interest, the more the American system deteriorates. This is the genesis of the real business cycle that causes boom and bust in the American system. Corporate interest cannot expect to be successful at the expense of the people without paying a heavy price. Yet the scale always bends more and more in the direction of big business until the people can no longer afford their products. Then there is bust. Big business must have the cooperation of people with purchasing power to continue their own growth. People without purchasing power cannot sustain capitalist economic growth. So it is in the best interest of corporations to contribute toward little people achieving economic success. Incredibly enough, one by one, individually, business will not and does not recognize this fact. Apparently, each is waiting for the other to take on this responsibility they individually don't want. That is why allowing business to usurp government power the way it has now is always a disaster. They will never, without government coercion, take on their share of responsibility to see that there is a fair balance between the interests of people and business.

Yet, in most of the history of America, business needs have been the dominant concern of lawmakers. Unless we can find some way to strike a balance between the needs of business and people our system will continue the same pattern as in the past. We have barely survived this tormented system in the past and I think it is totally unacceptable for the future. The only way our system can avoid the unsavory prospects of the business cycle is if we make reforms that will strike a balance between the supply side and the demand side of our economic system. The supply side is business activity and the demand side is people's purchasing power, including government, which is supposed to represent the people, not ears. We must reform our system, now. It is a disaster in its present manifestation.

The mission of this book is to try to show-how, by government always acting as an effective counterbalancing force, such a balance can be struck. Some people say that is what we have been trying to do. What we have been trying to do, though, is something completely different, as will be pointed out. We cannot do anything properly, however, unless we cure ourselves of pseudo democracy. In order to accomplish this we need to set up a true democratic challenge, such as a guarantee of full employment for every American. Government would then be forced by law to see that the industrial base is developed sufficiently to employ everyone who wants to be employed. This one act would mandate a balance of sorts in our system. That we could accomplish this and even much more if we really wanted to is my firm belief. The way to get there is expanded upon in this book. With true cooperation between government, the people and business - rather than the adversary relationship that now exists - America can become a real democracy. Anyone who thinks this is not true is sadly lacking in faith in the American people and the future.

The human race has just scratched the surface of its possibilities. There is unlimited energy locked up in the secrets of nature, just waiting to be tapped. Man's technology will soon make most kinds of work as it is now known obsolete. We must now begin to prepare for a completely new kind of world. A utopian like world that will surpass in its incredibility anything the imagination of man has ever envisioned. Technology has just begun to flower. Tomorrow's world has no limits. It is approaching at warp speed. As Franklin Roosevelt so wisely said, "The only thing we have to fear is fear itself." And I have to add, we do have to fear incompetent stupidity exhibited by world leaders who think the problems of the world can be solved out of the barrel of a gun or with nuclear bombs. Stupid is something to really fear, because it is the only thing that can guarantee our self-destruction. The way the world is now headed is plumb dumb. We are in a new arms race that cannot have any beneficial outcome for any party. The use by any party of a nuclear weapon will result in whole countries being annihilated back to the Stone Age. In the U.S. political expediency has replaced science when there is a choice between greed and the public good based on science. This is very stupid, because most of the riches of the future will be created by science and there will be more than enough to go around. Science is capable of solving all of our problems except our pig-headed inability to rule ourselves properly. We are still living in a politically corrupt stone age in comparison with the evolvement of technology. We must bring our intelligence to bear on the problem of human cooperation, the first reason for human beings banding together into communities. When we create a viable system of political equality and liberty, we can expect that the proper use of our resources by science will solve all the problems necessary to create heaven on earth. That we believe is the real purpose and reward of man on earth when he learns to properly live in peace with his fellow man. We hope here that we can contribute some ideas that may save us not only from a hell of war and economic collapse, but on a more positive note, lead us to a utopia of true democracy that will empower every human being to live the good life.

Chapter 2.

Who were the Incas?

The Incas were a hereditary ruling cast of nobility claiming immortal descent from the sun. They had ruled the Inca Empire for several hundred years prior to the arrival of and their subsequent conquest by the Spaniards in the early 1500's. The Inca empire stretched for over 3000 miles along the western coast of South America, from Ecuador in the north to Chile in the south, and to the eastern slopes of the Andes Mountains touching on the rain forests and jungles of the Amazon basin.

The Incas were similar to most other ancient dynasties in their despotic political sway over their subjects. Their uniqueness lay in a benevolent egalitarian economic system that guaranteed every one of their commoner subjects a bottom line of equality that ensured a certain amount of prosperity to everyone. The economic mechanism that ensured a continual balance in the equality of the common man was a perennial redistribution of land among the folk. Every year all land in the Inca Empire was divided equally among all the common people, including the newly conquered peoples. The government of the Incas was also way ahead of Andrew Jackson, who, for the first time in American history used federal government funds to make local improvements in the 1830's. The Incas fostered road building and terraced agriculture before the arrival of the white man that in development, efficiency and productivity, has never been surpassed in this most difficult of geographic regions, even in modern times. Their roads stretched for three thousand miles over some of the most difficult terrain in the world. They employed a method of terracing some of the steepest and highest mountains in the world - farming all the way from nearly sea level up to the barren frozen tundra of the Andes Mountains. Because of these changing altitudes, they were able to cultivate an incredible diversity of products. Many of our vegetable and fruit staples were first cultivated in this area. If for no other reason than that extreme poverty and starvation, two of humanities worst scourges, did not exist in this kingdom, the Incas can be said to have been in possession of one of the richest, most fruitful and well ruled civilizations ever to exist in the history of the world.

When the Spanish arrived in the early 1500's, they thought they had found the proverbial El Dorado because they found huge caches of silver and gold objects of veneration openly displayed in the courts of important religious sites. The Inca rulers, called Incas, were considered to be sons of the sun, the entity they venerated as God. Gold and silver, because of their color and reflective power, were in some way considered to be possessions or relations of the sun, and were venerated as such. The elite also adorned themselves in these metals as a mark of their hierarchical noble position. The Spaniards, bent on conquest in spite of being hopelessly outnumbered, followed the example of Cortez in Mexico and treacherously captured the powerful Inca, after being welcomed as beneficent Gods by the gullible natives. Curiosity killed the cat and the ancient rulers of the Incas. The pious Spaniards, in order to reform and save these savages from their pagan religion, kidnapped the Inca and demanded that his life be ransomed by his Indian subjects. The price - their humongous hoard of pagan gold and silver objects of worship. The Inca, who was the monarch over one of the greatest empires in the world, agreed to the ransom terms of the Spanish and he and his subjects gave up their most precious possessions to save his life. Unfortunately for the Inca, this pusillanimous maneuver did not save his life. The perfidious Spanish had learned too well the lesson of Mexico. Destroy the absolute ruler and you own the country.

After the Spanish finished sacking and pacifying the Inca empire of its accumulated wealth, they colonized and catholicized it. They replaced the native system of government with European reforms resulting in the institutions of power becoming the church, the Spanish king and private ownership on the model of European nations. Prominent among these early economic reforms were the enslavement of the Indians. Apparently the salvation of one's soul was not enough to qualify one for economic salvation in the eyes of the rapacious Spanish. The Indians became Christian slaves forced to build churches where once stood their temples. The once prosperous, efficient, benevolent economic system quickly declined into a subsistence economy characterized by the extreme poverty and malnutrition that exists in these regions to this day. The fine system of terraces are for the most part history. The economic system based on equal ownership of the land has been replaced by the predatory system of survival of the fittest. Would not the people of this part of the world have been better off for the last 500 years under the rule of the Incas and their benevolent despotism, rather than the free enterprise European private ownership that replaced it? Would there have been the starvation and misery that has since been the lot of the

Indians in these regions? Was Incaism any better than modern communism?

Probably not, but I think the Inca system, whatever name is appropriate, was superior to the freebooting, enslaving system that replaced it. To support the people who have lived well in these regions over the last five centuries millions have suffered from extreme poverty. As far as Incaism being similar to communism socialism, its philosophy centered on a religious component missing from the practice of communism, although economically it did very much resemble communism. I am sure that the downside of this authoritarian system was as unfortunate in many ways for the people of the Inca kingdom, as it has been for the recent "kingdoms" of communism. The similarities are fairly obvious. While the Incas had an egalitarian economic system for the common man that guaranteed a bottom line of security so that no one had to fear extreme poverty, it was a class society ruled by one absolute despotic ruler. The ruling class saw it as a duty to allow the common man enough prosperity to satisfy his basic material needs. Gold and other precious objects were reserved for religious observance and adornment of the ruling elite. In the recent Soviet Union there was a very similar system. The common man could expect to live a secure life free from any extreme of poverty, but the luxuries of life were mostly reserved for the ruling caste of bureaucrats. These bureaucrats understood that it was a duty of their caste to provide the common man all of the necessities of life that included adequate medical care. A total despot and his close advisors ruled the country. He was just as much an absolute monarch as was the ancient Inca. As did the egalitarian system of the Incas in the form of work for the state, the Soviet state that owned the means of production considered the surplus value (Net profit after recouping of production costs) of the workers as profit belonging to the state and used most of that surplus to support an expensive war machine to compete for world domination against the West. Notice, though, those rulers taking much of the surplus value created by workers and using it to support a war machine is exactly what capitalist democracy has been coming to under recent Republican régimes. And communism under the current Chinese regime has transformed from an equalitarian system similar to the high point of Russian communism to the ultimate capitalist corporatism, exploiting its workers to the point of virtual slavery.

Of course, in the time of the Inca Empire there was no "-isms" as we know "-isms" today. The Inca Empire represented a pragmatic partnership between the rich and the poor that was an extension of man's instinct or need to cooperate. The reason I find the Inca system so interesting is that this extreme contrast of cooperation between aristocracy and peasants contradicts a concept we have today -

a black or white concept like so much of our thinking - that supposes an economic-social-political system has to be either a totally predatory capitalist system or a wholly oppressive communist system. And socialism, in contrast to its theory, is in practice playing a role toward the center of the other two ideologies. Of course, the people who favor these ideologies represent themselves as being in favor of either one extreme or the other of these systems and are not suggesting any alternative that might frighten off their followers, even if it is a better choice. However, radical changes are being made without the followers being informed.

The Inca system suggests a middle ground between the every person for themselves anarchy of extreme capitalism and the repressive centralization of communism. It strongly suggests the possibility of an alternative, because it demonstrates that even the extreme opposites of monarchy and socialism can work beneficially in the same system. I am convinced that capitalism and socialism can and are successfully meshing in a synthesis – and both will be better off for it. China is now proving this to be true economically, if not politically and humanely. How this can be done democratically and humanely even better and worldwide is the main objective of this book. There is no question that the Incas had a very effective government based on an organic harmony between monarchy and collective socialism. It would have been a lot more like true socialism if the surplus fruits of man's labor would not have been confiscated by the monarchy for ostentatious religious and hierarchical purposes. The point here, I hope not tormented to meaningless gibberish, is that Incaism demonstrated that a combination of crude free enterprise for the rich and crude socialism for the poor could work to everyone's benefit perhaps better than either alone. Certainly, the common people were more valuable to the monarchy as taxable subjects and loyal warriors rather than people who would be downtrodden and starving beggars otherwise. The European system put in place since the Spanish conquest has not worked well for the indigenous people for the last five hundred years; however, it now seems that some of the currently elected governments in the region may be reverting to the socialist extreme of the Inca equation. I think we have reached a point in the evolution of the human race where there is a valuable lesson to be learned from this great experiment in government.

The idea of this book is certainly not to make a case for a benevolent despotism based on the Inca model because despotism of any kind is only good as long as there is a good ruler. (See Tom Payne on monarchy for an apt description) Rulers that are not subject to the rule of law cannot be prevented from doing what they do best, abusing power. One Caligula or Hitler or Stalin, or even an elected incompetent president can undo in a day all the good it may have taken the sacrifices of millions of lives many years to bring about. Hitler's despotism was, in a sense, democratic despotism, since he was elected (Albeit with thugs waiting in the wings to frighten) democratically by the majority and brought to power by the majority, albeit a small one. Democracy is not a guaranteed panacea against tyrants if it does not protect minority rights. Therefore, all forms of despotism are dangerous, with majority despotism probably more dangerous than the rest because you cannot cut off the head and expect the tail to shrivel up and die. The Third Reich's campaign to destroy what were to them worthless minorities demonstrated this better than any words. The handicapped, Jehovah's Witnesses, Jews, Gypsies, socialists/communists, gays, unionists, influential religious leaders and other minorities were all targets of their evil death machine. This democratically elected tyrant Hitler proved to be the worst scourge of minorities in human history.

The idea of this book is not to emulate the Inca system, but to take inspiration from the ancient Incas, concluding that a benevolent democratic egalitarian economic-political-social system can be created out of the combination of the most extreme, common, or even esoteric elements. If the ancient Inca despots could create prosperity and equality for the masses, there is no excuse for the richest nation in the world not to be able to create security for its citizens. Free enterprise capitalism should back a bottom line socialistic security for the masses not interested in becoming entrepreneurial individualists. Economic security for the little person will cause there to be an economic climate in which everyone will have a chance to make money without feeling guilty about ripping off his neighbor to prosper. Anyone who is not a hypocrite knows that our exploitative system boils down to a basic ethic that is: "Rip off your neighbor before he rips you off". The opposite of Jesus Christ's wise teachings. We must grow up and out of such a childish philosophy of life. We are only visiting this spaceship for a very short period of time and it is stupid to think it is possible to spiritually fulfill a life in this span of time by an endless selfish greedy quest to accumulate wealth. This reduction of greed to the spiritual absurd seems to suggest that the point of life may be quite different than an endless quest to make more money. Even those of us who are agnostically inclined and don't know what to believe spiritually, can find an eternal purpose in growing and developing so that we can go on to do better things if called upon.

If we deny our neighbors, however distant, the right to the key to eternal life - developing and growing as human beings - we are taking away both freedom and eternity from them. We cannot take what the Gods alone have the right to give and not be punished for it. The concept of eternal fulfillment is implied in the individual rights and responsibilities of real democracy. The Creator has given the right to fulfillment to humanity as the greatest gift of all, Whomsoever and Whatsoever the Creator may be. Even if the Creator is only human wishful thinking alone, man's evolving technology is clearly leading him toward eternal life. If this is true, as it surely is, certainly eternal life must be a possibility somewhere in this vast universe of ours. Everyone should have the opportunity to participate. And everyone should pull together to make this possible. Woe to the despots of the world who stand in the way of the right of humanity to eternal life. They will inherit the kingdom of hell on Earth.

Enough of this fire and brimstone pontificating. On a more down to-earth level: we are going to have a bloody mess, as we have already had, if we do not find a way to speed up the true democratization of the world. We can if we try, create a truly democratic political system that is in various ways a mixture of socialism and capitalism, and that will of a certainty, be a vast improvement over either alone. This is already partially the case, but it needs to be better. We will attempt to show how true democracy means freedom for everyone, including entrepreneurs and workers. Despotism is a system wherein one class dominates and exploits another class. A pragmatic economic-political democracy guaranteeing the prosperity and individual rights of all its citizens, whether worker or capitalist entrepreneur would in all probability be the first true freedom to ever exist.

It is the strong contention in this book, that all attempts to achieve a truly democratic civilization have been dismal failures. We sometimes make the mistake of thinking that the word "republic", which is representative government, and "democracy" mean the same thing. They do not! However, because these two terms for different kinds of government are used inter-changeably, what we call democracy has often erroneously become synonymous with economic despotism! It is the thesis of this book that the present failure of all political systems in the world to bring about the widespread happiness of mankind is the failure of real democracy to truly flower.

Often in history slaves have been better fed, clothed, and housed than their so-called free counterparts. Many people under the prison camp company town system of the Soviet Union were better off materially than millions of free men in the so-called free world. But, no man or woman is happy feeling he is a slave or a prisoner. Given the opportunity, most men and women would choose to risk all for freedom; even, if as is often the case, the only thing free about the word freedom is the word itself. Freedom should be bestowed on all men and women as a right of birth. Nowhere is this the case. Freedom can only be bought, often at the price of a soul: for to be truly free means to be able to choose your own destiny without making compromises. Or compromising the freedom of your neighbor! It means the right to fulfill yourself to the best of your abilities. And it means that if each and every one of your fellow citizens does not have the same right, you are participating in a conspiracy to deprive your fellow citizen of his or

her right to freedom. By the law of karma, also known as the law of cause and effect, we all share equally in the sins of the world.

To give a man an education, a job, bread, clothes, shelter and a bank account does not make him free. It also does not define a society as democratic, as some countries would have their citizens - not to mention the rest of the world - believe. To have the right to vote does not make a man or woman free or define a society as democratic, as our leaders in America would have us believe. We are children of the universe and we must have room to grow.

And, of course, the world knows we are free, the favorite mantra of American politicians. This Orwellian 1984 style newspeak and doublethink grew apace with the recent Republican ascendancy and decadency. The moral Majority that turned out to be an immoral minority, turned into a Republican revolution that has been a reactionary farce, and turned into a nightmare of radicalism that was successfully converting everything traditionally American into rubbish until its recent overthrow. There was nothing, as it claims, conservative about it and it was preeminently corrupt. The ones who were in charge in America, circa 2006, claiming the label of Republican conservatives, in a word, were smart crooks. The Nazis were also smart crooks, freely elected. That such people can come to power in a so-called democracy is a glaring flaw of representative government that makes possible what I define as pseudo-democracy. This is a flaw that can only be corrected by creating genuine democracy.

George Orwell's 1984 system of government based on twisting the truth into its opposite, is now, and always has been, with us. Politicians call themselves conservatives when they are radicals and sheep when they are wolves and many people naively believe them. Practically every society today considers itself a democracy in some way and none really are, while the predators of every nation arm themselves at will and prepare for the final holocaust - all paid for by the people. Yes, George Orwell certainly hit the mark. We are being worded, as Shakespeare might say, by words that are like old friends.

You are so pleased to see them you would never dream that perhaps they are not the same people they once were. We have spent thousands of years, with the patience of the blissfully ignorant, building a civilization that is on the verge of harnessing infinite, as opposed to finite, knowledge. As the old saying goes, a little knowledge is dangerous. Man has proven this to be true over and over with ever more destructively mindless wars that always utilize the latest technological innovation to kill in greater and greater numbers. A lot of knowledge is proving to be a lot more dangerous. With almost infinite technology at hand, we have the capacity to destroy everyone on the planet. There are already acclaimed scientists, such as lizard expert E.R. Pianka, appalled by man's depredation of the earth, who in order to save it, seriously propose reducing the population of the earth by ninety percent. Don't laugh, because the technology to do this is out there already. Our present domestic leadership is for the most part a pack of poorly educated ignoramuses who got where they are by successfully deceiving us the people into thinking they reflect our views. The politicians in power today in America have proven themselves to be incompetent for the jobs they are in. If we do not soon learn how to choose honest intelligent life oriented people as our leaders, we might as well pack it in, because we now live in a world that can be destroyed by one foolish politician in a moment. Or in just a little more time, a mad scientist with a genetically enhanced germ like an air born Ebola or bird flu, will probably have the tools to kill us all with impunity. We still haven't caught the anthrax killer, remember?

Chapter 3

What is real democracy?

Democracy is probably the most misused word in the human tongue. According to Webster's dictionary, democracy is a form of government for the people, by the will of the majority of the people, and based on the concept of the equality of man. One could not have a very good idea of what democracy is from this definition. The first concept in this definition, "for the people", seems to be dependent on the good will of that mentioned in the second concept, the majority, even though the majority may decide, as it did, to elect the National Socialist Party of Adolph Hitler. So, a mad criminal does not determine what is good for the people, like Adolph or another individual, but by the majority, which, if it so chooses, may elect lemmings to run the country.

This implies that democracy could, if the majority so decided, be an annual trip to the Pacific Ocean where, instead of sunbathing, we would all have to drown ourselves. If, however, this were to be true democracy according to Webster we would obey the admonition of proposition three and drown ourselves equally. There are those, as there always will be, cynical souls, however, who might add that the only true equality willed by the majority is the right to drown together. We know, from our experience in Vietnam, where the burden of the war was carried by the underprivileged, that some men are more equal than others. Proposition three, then, is limited by what the majority perceives to be the equality of man, which frequently resembles nothing close to equality.

The majority will then is not limited to the choices open to it, usually based on the constitution and/or other traditions such as our amendments to the constitution, congressional laws and the attitudes of the courts, because everything is open to biased interpretation. Thus, not only can the majority will be interpreted freely according to its own prejudices and biases, but the courts may even, legitimatize these prejudices by imposing its own biases. The courts may even impose a minority will on the country such as was done when it appointed George W. Bush as President without a fair review of the Florida vote count. So, at least in the case of American democracy, if the constitutional guarantees of specific rights for the individual are not clearly delineated, democracy can be limited by the courts, the President or Congress: limited to a shadow, cosmetic or pseudo democracy reflecting their own biases and prejudices more than the views of the people. And this is the case as respect to the present Bush 2 administration, as reflected by polls showing people do not support the administrations agenda in most of their proposals, excepting those concerning national security. If all the tenets of a contract are compromised, there is no contract. If there is no social contract, there is no democracy. If, then, there is such a thing as real democracy, what is it? It may surprise some people to learn that the USSR, when it existed, and other communist states then as now consider themselves to be democracies. This is in spite of the fact that "the majority" in those kinds of states accounted for less than five percent of the population who constituted 100% of the party in power. This kind of majority is actually a ruling minority, belonging to the only party these countries allow, the communist party. These communist countries have constitutions much like other constitutions, piously mandating most of the human rights mandated in most constitutions. The constitution of some of these countries has been changed and upgraded sometimes many times to improve their "democracy". China's latest constitutional upgrade, in my view, unnoticed by the world, made it possible to change from a socialist to a capitalist country. And that is what has taken place virtually without comment by the world press or other governments. In one important way the constitutions of communist countries have been honored much as the constitutions of traditional western democracies have been; sanctimoniously to the letter when it has been convenient for the people in power, often in the breech when it has not been. Bush 2 may be the most obvious such offender in U.S. history, but not the first.

Constitutionally mandated equality under the Soviet democratic system was perceived to be a classless society in which the surplus value - the surplus fruits of men's labor - was supposed to be enjoyed by all citizens equally. The end result was supposed to be a kind of utopian society where the state withered away, and mankind achieved the ultimate freedom to choose from the common store whatever he needed. How close did Soviet communist humanity come to the realization of this idealized equality in the over 70 years the Bolsheviks were in power? As close as a prison camp or mental institution, according to the survivors of this utopian experiment. It is alleged that since World War II the Soviet Union, in spite of a constitution that contained humanely democratic wording, enslaved and worked over twenty million people to their deaths. The authorities in the beginning justified this historically unprecedented mass holocaust of its own citizens by claiming these people were dangerous political dissenters. It later became just an excuse to supply slave labor, mostly for highly profitable mining and construction projects in places where it was a virtual death sentence to have to work. And millions of innocent people were worked to death in these awful labor camps under the banner of national security. Certainly democracy in the Soviet Union did not make provision for freedom to dissent, except possibly on paper. A dissenter would soon find himself in a gulag. The rest of the country, surviving in a climate of insane paranoid fear, had developed into one vast company town kind of lifestyle. Russia, it seems, had become the antithesis of its ideology. It had become the ideal monopoly corporation, for want of a better definition. Its bureaucratic departments were comparable to the hundreds of subsidiaries of GE or other large corporations. And like them, it took the surplus value (Once promised to workers) of the workers for their labor and spent it according to the dictates of the board of directors, represented by the Communist Party politburo. Like any other corporation, it sought to expand and protect its own interests with little regard for the needs and preferences of the people who produced the wealth. It was a despotic system of state socialist monopoly capitalism, pure and simple. They achieved the ultimate capitalist monopoly by having the power to totally exploit the workers who only could complain if they wanted to end up in a gulag. And this was called the dictatorship of the proletariat. What a laugh. This political system, which claimed to be communist democracy, was neither politically democratic nor economically socialism. And it was not communism as envisioned by Karl Marx, either. It was pure unbridled monopoly capitalist corporatism in the sense that workers had no say in the distribution of the wealth they created or any say in anything for that matter. Why then did it fail? The short answer is incompetent management.

The surplus value generated by Russian workers was largely squandered on competing in a world-class arms race instead of creating a competitive world-class peacetime economy. It bankrupted itself in this foolish pursuit that could not be justified by its economic base. It was further discredited because non-military products of its economy were of such very poor quality that no one wanted them. Russian workers had very little to choose from even from the poor choices available because of an infamously disastrous distribution system. The workers had no choice about almost anything in their lives. Their life style was almost totally dictated by the Communist party. It was not, however, the dictatorship of the proletariat (Worker): it was the dictatorship of a corporate bureaucracy that only thinks of a worker as one cost factor in a product made for one reason only, profit. It was 1984 with Big Brother in full charge. If the Soviet Union's leaders actually believed democracy is what existed in their country, they deserved the Nobel idiot prize for their twisted understanding of the term. But, that is exactly what they thought of it as. Human denial knows no bounds of self-deluding stupidity. Who can imagine a free people exercising its majority will making a choice to live under such a system? What people would freely choose an economic model that did not provide enough consumer goods to keep people's money from rotting in the bank? The Soviet experiment in so called Communism exhibited better than any other the danger of any kind of dictatorial domination, minority or majority, without effective checks on power. Unless every human being's rights are protected every other human being is in dire jeopardy of having his freedom undermined. The rhetoric of "dictatorship of the proletariat" turned into pure dictatorship and gross incompetent use of power. Such rhetoric should never have been used in connection with a system claiming to be socialism or democracy in the first place.

An unfortunate system of two parties that are substantively different only in the way with which they fool the public has become the monopoly political animal in he United States. The two political parties in America should, for the sake of honesty and clarity, be re-named Conservative and Radical. The democrats are clearly the real conservatives trying to preserve a liberal agenda that had become an entrenched position for over 50 years until the Republican revolution of Newt Gingrich that was truly a right wing revolution. It was a revolution, because it has sold the American people on the idea that radical departure from the liberal tradition since Roosevelt is real conservatism. In fact, it is only *radical*. And it is mainly radical in the sense that it has changed the masters from whom it receives its financial support. Of course new masters usually have a new agenda to be advocated. This is the other change. Therefore the Republican Party is the Radical Party in reality because it represents a new global reality not to the best advantage of America. And it is a very clever advocate indeed. It evolved from Reagan's simple-minded conservative agenda, but subtly metamorphosized. It's big lie has

been to preempt the word conservative that masks its total sell out of
the American electorate it is supposed to represent, to the interests of
the transnational corporations, the new masters. Conservative my
foot! They are using the doublethink device of George Orwell (Mental
flip-flop cheating) to legitimatize a radical departure from American
economic values that have traditionally protected American workers.
Its first big perceivable mistake may be starting a financially ruinous
un-winnable war mainly in order to obtain corporate access for the
multi-national Halliburton Corporation and others to Iraq's oil
industry. This has done more to unmask its deceit than anything else.

Politicians who erroneously think of themselves as representing
liberal or conservative polarities presently dominate both parties. This
loss of touch with reality contributes to a public distortion of
perception that the democrats are weak and inept tax and spenders and
that the Republicans are tough, but efficient tax cutters. Whether part
of this may be true or not, it is more likely that due to the fact that
both parties are outmoded by agendas that are inappropriate for what
is needed now to solve America's problems, there is a cast a plague on
both your houses mentality by many voters who refuse to vote. The
prospects of American politicians satisfying the American people's

needs is badly failing and the American people and everyone but the politicians know it, either consciously or intuitively. It is past due time to change this drastically outmoded system.

Senator Ted Kennedy, one of the few politicians who has not dropped his weapons and run for the nearest exit to get out of the way of the Republican stampede, has called the Republicans "the religion of inaction". Another of his famous sound bites is calling a Republican budget "patent medicine that is supposed to cure all economic ills in three swallows". The power of language can be used for or against the best interests of the people. A great character defect of the America people is that we expect instant cures for all ills. The Republicans know this and use it very effectively in their rhetoric, as Bush recently did in reference to the Iraq war. It has allowed them to sell the public on globalization, privatization, smaller government and tax cuts as the panacea for all problems even though in almost all cases these things are detrimental to the vast majority of the population.

Once in power, both parties have demonstrated that they represent only one segment of the population, even though they claim otherwise. The one class always represented in America is the "haves", defined as the rich owner class and to a lesser degree, powerful unions representing well-heeled workers. The real difference between the two parties is the difference between the subtle person and the blunt person. It is the difference between broadminded enlightenment and dogmatic traditional narrow mindedness. It is, in the final analysis, the difference between compassionate, subtle, enlightened, conservative benevolence of the left and uncompassionate blunt, arrogant, selfish radical usurpation of democratic principles by the right. However different the modus operandi of the liberal Republican or Democrat and the conservative Republican or Democrat - and their modus operandi is quite different - the overall aim is almost the same: to fool the electorate into believing this individual best commiserates with their interests. If this were not the truth, an ultra-liberal like George McGovern could never have been elected time after time in a highly conservative state like South Dakota. It is just that an intelligent electorate perceives that, "What is in the name of a rose? A rose by any other name might stink worse. I'll take the rose that smells OK even if he is the wrong label". And if a leader who purports to represent them convinces them he is on their side by putting a lot of pork on the table, they will stick with him no matter his label. The people, who are certainly smarter than rats, have been hoodwinked into abandoning the sinking rotten liberal ship only to jump into shark infested right wing waters. Now they are being told their life rafts are leaky and should be privatized. When they realize this too is a scam, they will probably jump ship again, as has recently happened. Can this be the harbinger of the end of democracy, as we now know it? We think so. Let us hope the change is not the one made in ancient Rome, from republic to empire. However, the plutocrats of multi-nationalist corporations are sitting in the wings waiting. They already have gone to Caesar CEO's. How else can you explain the plundering by the CEO's? What ever happened to the legal concept of fiduciary trust to the stockholders? That item seems to be missing from the corporate table.

The Democrats operate on about the same level as those leaders of ancient Rome who bought the people's affections with games and corn and a drachma or two. I do not know or care if this system had a name in ancient Rome, but in modern times, it is known as the dole. Its main purpose is to help the impoverished people find a life raft to survive in the undertow that is modern free enterprise. The liberal dole, even though it has provided basic necessities for the poor, has done very little to save the poor from poverty, anyway, according to various voices that oppose it. One of the myths about the American way of life currently being shattered by current social historians that the New Deal, out of which modern liberal prestige grew, seriously improved the conditions of the poor. The fact is that New Deal policies mainly helped the middle and upper classes, with the status of the poor remaining about the same. Upward mobility is another American myth. Recent studies show that the vast majority of people in the U.S. tend to stay in their respective class. The fact is New Deal policies and the war economy of W.W. II saved the middle class from poverty that, in all probability, would have otherwise ended in real revolution. The middle and upper classes will not stand for the same punishment they mete out to the poor. The poor are supposed to be poor so the rich can identify themselves and have cheap labor. The self-anointed conservative Republicans believe, deep in their hearts, in survival of the fittest. This world is an imagined jungle paradise to them, because their consciences are assuaged by the myth that it is fair and egalitarian when every man, woman, child and old person has an equal chance to become king of the beasts and devour his fellow man. Is it any wonder that with such a monstrous socio-economic philosophy the dominating ethic of the community, that murder and rape have become an everyday occurrence? Murder and rape are only a natural extension of a philosophy that states that man should live by preying on his fellow man. The idea of brotherly love is as foreign to a Republican conservative as it is to a sleazy mugger. They would both be right at home eating you for dinner if this were a real jungle. They are deluding themselves if they think they have anything in common with the ethical values of the founders of great religious movements of which they most likely are members. The problem is they don't think. Is it any wonder that men and women in America today more often hunt each other like prey than seek each other as companions in the fulfillment of life? When you consider the consequences, this radical predatory ethos is an inhumane spiritual void that reduces everyman to the level of a beast of prey. Loveless predatory sex leads to auto-genocide of the practitioner, because he fails to reproduce. This in turn leads to a breakdown in the whole fabric of society and finally the state. In order for a society to maintain its cultural identity and evolve, it must reproduce. The Western world by adapting an auto-genocidal ethos has doomed its culture to dead end self-destruction unless it soon wakes up. Nature hates a vacuum and the Muslims are filling it. This is the plain truth.

These two forces of liberal and conservative push and pull at each other as though they were archenemies, which in fact they believe themselves to be. Actually, their goal is the same: to protect what is not a vanishing species - the human birds of prey. Politics in America is like a grandfather's clock with a pendulum swinging backwards and forwards. It is a grand ole machine that never goes anywhere but backward and forward. But time marches on. The world is changing and evolving all around us, and time is running out if we want to set the pace as we always have in America. The digital watch, thanks to research paid for by the people, has replaced the grandfather's clock, but our politicians promise us a new deal every four years and we always end up with a raw deal. Something is wrong and nobody knows what it is. We go on electing politicians more out of habit and frustration than out of rational belief in their promises. I hope in these pages to offer some antidotes to a political system that has degenerated to the point that it is turning the American dream into the American nightmare.

The present Bush administration represents discredited ideas of the federalists in an attempt to turn the clock back to ideas that are as doomed to failure today as they were in Jefferson's time. The Republican supply side economics is a new theory for an old Republican election scam to promise economically beneficial tax cuts any time it will win them elections. This is a perversion of Keynesian economic pump priming it is based on. They know that any tax cut at any time will stimulate the economy and use it to claim economic success without regard to the long-term debt that is created for the following generations to pay off. This is contrary to the Keynesian idea of priming the pump in bad times and paying the debt in good times. It is the Republican ace instant cure for everything because it is supposed to stimulate the economy and result in more tax revenue at the same time that we pay fewer taxes. Well, Clinton was able to create a surplus by opposite methods including balancing the budget. Harding and Coolidge's similar Republican policies had the result of great prosperity followed by the worst depression in history when Hoover arrived. Supply side economics is just a new term for old-time stale conservative Republican ideas of one-sided expansion of industry at the expense of everything else. Who is going to be able to buy this increased production if they keep allowing the degradation of jobs? As of 2006, the government says available jobs are growing by the millions, but what kind of jobs? Almost all are low paying menial service jobs! Of that, the government's perfidious spin machine doesn't inform you. It intentionally is under informing you. And the shallow minded conglomerate owned media, with few exceptions, seems incapable of digging in and exposing the truth of distorted spun reports. No wonder people are unable to vote intelligently. The American media is much better about blowing the whistle on other countries. Margaret Thatcher had been in office in Great Britain for two years and her "economic miracle" based on conservative policies similar to Reagan's at the time was a colossal fizzle. Great Britain, in spite of being self sufficient in oil, still had high inflation and unemployment, as high as during the Great Depression. (April 24, 1981 L.A. Times; "British unemployment reached the highest level in 50 years, since April 1931. 10.4% of the work force and 2.5 million workers unemployed.") Great Britain and America, in spite of so many differences, have one very similar problem. When there is an economic problem, they cannot make up their minds what is really wrong or, therefore, how to go about fixing it. My guess is that, because the rulers cannot except that anything is fundamentally wrong, they refuse to see the problem.

The first, but by no means the whole problem in America is that the basic health of democracy has been undermined and destroyed by the ascendancy of an undemocratic, inhumane economic despotism that has the capacity to impose its will on the majority, no matter what party is elected to office. The people in the United States, who are charged with the responsibility of choosing leaders from parties and candidates that claim to represent them in their campaign rhetoric, are so divided, uninformed, befuddled, and misled that they do not know their own best interests. Campaign rhetoric, as Ronald Reagan once admitted, is synonymous with lying, but people still haven't woke up to that fact. The reason the American people do not know their own best interest has much to do with the confusion over what democracy really stands for. The American people have been hyped on the mythical ethic that America has solely been made great by the great capitalist individualist and can only be great in the future if powerful entrepreneurs are enabled that can create new job expanding businesses. The idea suggested is that, if only we had more of the old individualist entrepreneurial spirit, prosperity would be achieved for everyone. This is fine in theory, but it does not account for the fact that everyone is not of a competitive nature or equipped by training, age, or numerous other reasons to be competitive. Also, there are many important jobs that require a high degree of skill and training that are relatively low paying simply because they do not offer the opportunity to be selfish, greedy, and grasping, like teaching. The biggest problem of all is that it is total hypocrisy to preach the individualist spirit when globalization has in many ways made the individual entrepreneur as obsolete as the Dodo Bird. Many of the business opportunities that used to be open to entrepreneurs have been preempted by global corporate competition. It takes entrepreneurs to start corporations also, but corporations are not inhabited by individualists, but by team playing bureaucrats.

In America we are proud of our Horatio Algers who often with little or no skills or education, have amassed empires worth millions and billions of dollars. Some of these have been unconscionable predators who have been little better than criminals. That little better makes all the difference, however. I am not saying there is anything wrong with making a lot of money. What is wrong is the perverse value that the man, who by luck, inheritance, shrewdness or hard work happens to be a captain of industry and worth a lot of money, is hailed as a hero and responsible for the greatness of America; while the people who work for him and have made it possible for him to be successful, the non-individualist silent majority of workers would, by the above definition of American greatness, be considered to have contributed little or nothing to America's greatness. Americans, then, have been hyped on an inferiority complex, especially female and black Americans, because everyone knows that Mr. Entrepreneurial Moneybags knows best what is right for America, because he is the only real individualist. Money and righteousness go hand in hand in the American people's minds. We do not think there is any proof, at this stage in our history, that anyone knows what is best for this country.

In America, then, the simplest basic economic definition of democracy is not equality, but selfish individualism, democratic capitalism if you will. How did this metamorphosis of principles come about? The answer is simple. We never have had equality in America. We do not have a tradition of anything even resembling equality. Therefore, we have never had anything even resembling real democracy in America. Our constitution does not guarantee equality, it guarantees representative government. It was drawn up at an idealistic time in our history when, in spite of our desire to ban the abuses of despotism from which we had been suffering, we were not ready to create genuine democracy because our economic system was not based on equality. In fact, probably more than half the people in the country were either black slaves or indentured white servants - another form of slavery. The question is, are we ready for democracy now, or is the ideal of democracy-equality a vanishing species like elected liberals? (Before the current 06 mid-term elections. However many of those demos elected were conservatives) One thing is for certain; contrary to popular myth, current social historians have demonstrated that equality in America has been on the decline throughout the entire history of the Republic. Yet the general standard of living has been increasing fairly consistently over the long run – giving the illusion of increased equality. But in real terms, the gap is always widening between the rich and the poor. In other words, we have been getting richer instead of getting equal. We must, then, ask the question, should equality necessarily be a basic tenet of real democracy? Our answer is yes, but not equality as it is now defined. Our definition of equality will be based on what empowerment level of help an individual should receive in order to empower that individual to have an equal chance of fulfillment in life. In simpler real terms, equal opportunity as opposed to absolute equality.

Democracy in America is popularly thought of as the mandates of our constitution, our amendments including the Bill of Rights, and the laws passed by our various representative governments. It is taken for granted that these laws are democratic and fair to everyone. Based on the guidelines, of the people, by the people, for the people, equal justice under the laws and protection of minority or individual rights, I think the result falls sadly short of real democracy. We have seen how, in the case of Abscam in the past and Duke Cunningham and Congressman Jefferson in the present, all you have to do, apparently, is offer any Congressman or Senator a bribe, usually in the form of a campaign contribution, and they will go to bat for your cause. Unfortunately, campaign contributions don't count as bribes. Is this ultimate free enterprise, when our elected representatives go into business for themselves? Certainly, on the basis of such evidence, they do not represent all the people. No wonder the surplus value of the American worker is being taken and handed over to the military-industrial-government complex to be squandered on stupidly botched wars like Vietnam and Iraq. One of the things little understood by the public is that the main object of American foreign policy under

all presidents has been to open new markets for business. That's what these wars are really about. There is nothing wrong with using the offices of the U.S. Government to help business prosper and gain new markets, but the combination of the military-industrial-government axis of evil has created a new dangerous incentive for what has turned out with the Iraq war to be pure economic adventurism. What is telltale about the truth of this is how the war has been pursued. It is obvious that everything is being done to avoid offending the population of Iraq as much as possible, no matter what the cost in lives of American soldiers. We want to win their hearts, minds, and oil permanently. The best proof of this is how the country is being rebuilt by requiring our troops to fight the war and rebuild the country at the same time. And this when there have never been enough troops to do one job right, let alone the other. Also, to me, another great irony is that, all the high profile trouble that was gone to at the beginning of the war to destroy the communications network, (Command and control) only to have it replaced by a foreign owned cell phone company that has been allowed to set up a network that is providing the insurgency with all the command and control it needs to regroup and attack our troops. And these phones are one of the main devices used to set off IED's that are killing and maiming most of our troops that are hurt. And this has never been, as of this writing, questioned anywhere publicly, either by the media or government officials to my knowledge. Is this stupidity or something more sinister like my above allegation? This in Nov. 2006 is incredible to me. It is obviously another example of the desperate attempt to keep the Iraq population friendly even at the price of killed and horribly maimed American soldiers. Whatever the real reason we are there, we should be fighting a lot smarter. The insurgents have found our Achilles heel and we are going to face this IED menace anywhere we go to war from now on. Iran probably has one every five feet along any invasion route.

If we have such one sided, special interest representation such as we have in congress, we do not even have representative government, let alone democracy. I think the biggest problem with democracy in America, as was mentioned before, is that people do not really know what their best interests are and often vote against their own best interests; true or not, the people's interests are supposed to come first.

This is clearly not the case in Washington. If the people's interests were paramount, the economic problem of high paying job depression, loss of manufacturing base, trade and budget deficits would at least be confronted and not shoved under the rug as they now are. We are clearly headed for disaster. The American electorate is not a bunch of sadomasochistic fruit cakes who enjoy spending the fruits of their labor to pay for a world order based on free trade for everybody but America. This pseudo free trade is guarded by America the superpower policeman, paid for by the American taxpayer, and benefited by the multi-national corporations. Whatever democracy really is, it is not a rape of the taxpayer in the name of national security and free trade. But that is what it is.

There is an interesting democratic model in Sweden that has accommodated a partnership between capitalism and socialism for many years under the figurehead auspices of a constitutional monarchy. Sweden has been for many years an extreme welfare state where people are taxed so heavily that there is a spread of no more than two and a half times between what the lowest paid worker earns and the highest. (And most Swedes do not mind this heavy taxation because they get a lot for their tax dollar) Taxation under the Swedish system of taxation is 50-60 percent individual, 28 percent corporate. Not so many years ago, Sweden had the highest per capita income and longest lifespan in the world. Everything went very well indeed as long as there was prosperity. Sweden subsequently, however, has had serious downturns that have threatened to unravel the whole fabric of their system. This was blamed on the high percentage of GDP transferred to the poor. They have managed with only minor adjustments to recover and save this system in spite of all challenges. There are many lessons to be learned from Sweden. Number one is that no system of government will be successful unless there is a healthy economic model in place that can support the level of social development that has been arrived at. And that model has to change with changing conditions.

When the Swedish economy began to falter some years back, Swedish economists came to believe their economy was faltering not because of some unknown mysterious problem or, as American economists believe, not at all, but because it had become non-competitive in the world marketplace. Without going into a comprehensive analysis of the Swedish system, let us say, that in terms of Republican tax cutter beliefs, Sweden should have collapsed long ago from a top-heavy burden of taxation that went largely to support their comprehensive social development. Contrary to this, Sweden has been, in spite of ups and downs, very successful economically over the long term when it has been able to maintain its competitiveness in the world market. It also, in spite of periodic economic turndowns, has been able to maintain with some social cutbacks its welfare state and its market economy at the same time. This has also been in spite of what is perhaps the highest practical taxation in the world. This seems to indicate that the problem of creating prosperity is a problem of competition, more than distribution of wealth. This then to me seems to be clue numero uno that we cannot have a stable world economy until we learn how to create fair world economic competition. The discussion and solution of this problem is the subject of another chapter. However, we believe this is the crux of a very mysterious situation in which the western economy is rapidly shrinking while the Asian economies are rapidly expanding. And many countries in the third world seem to have no chance of having a real economy at all. Not we believe, solely because of the usual suspects of corruption, instability, lack of education etc, but because there is little incentive for outside investors to risk capital in places that have the whole competitive deck stacked against them. The tigers of Asia had to start by drastically exploiting their workers with inhumane working conditions and low pay before they could begin to compete on a tech scale as they are now doing. The Chinese went so far as to change their constitution to make it possible for them to compete on a world scale, a little known fact. As a consequence, their workers are no longer guaranteed employment and are possibly the worst exploited in the world. This draconian reversal of employment laws has caused them to become a socialist state in name only, (The economic part of Communism is socialism), as America is a democracy in name only. Oh woe, how all the world is nothing but a big fat lie.

Democracy certainly is not defined as chronic underemployment, poverty or crime caused mostly by unemployment, class structure of have and have-nots, excessive regressive taxation that is punishing to poor people, military expenditures so excessive it subsidize economies that our own industry must compete with, and, government representing special interest groups more than the people. However, the negatives of pseudo democracy do not define real democracy. The level of equality of opportunity afforded the people defines real democracy.

Our military expenditures are a futile attempt to dominate a world no longer willing to be dominated by anything except ideas. Because of this dominance of ideas created by instant world inter-communications, democracy and/or any other ideology, must by good example, win the hearts and minds of people before it can expect to win their friendship. No system or ideology will be permanent until true democracy makes possible, by its example, the peaceful solution of the major problems facing the human race. The affections of countries cannot be finessed by the kind of military adventurism or bribery of despotic systems of government that used to be the dominant forces in world politics. During the cold war, as countries friendships were bought and sold by the highest bidder, the Soviets, as much as the U.S. had their hard little hearts broken by one or more hot romance turned sour. There is no longer an auction market for dominance of third world countries, except to corporations. Foreign governments are seen as colonists. Corporations are not, even if they really are.

If democratic societies want to have their principles permanently dominant in the world, they are going to have to make a commitment to a utopian future in which all humans will be reasonably rich (Similar to our middle class), fulfilled with at least the satisfaction of the Swedes, guaranteed decent employment or comparable compensation for not working, and in which the surplus value of workers needs to be shared fairly between employers, government and themselves; not appropriated to be wasted on wars or other nonsense. What should also be learned from the Swedish experiment is that there has to be balance. The government should not be committed to bankrupting itself entirely over social expenditures either, as the Swedes nearly did. The balancing needs of expanding the industrial base must be seen to wisely also or the whole organic system will break down. A welfare state, like any other state, should be viewed as an organic whole; a whole is only as good as the sum of its parts.

Foolishly expecting a desperate world to follow our example and copy our system of government, we are presently exhibiting an example of America that is an obscene absurdity of asswholian redneck anarchy. I apologize for this pompous flourish of alliterative grape shot worthy of Pat Buchanan speech writing for assorted crooks, but if winning the battle for the soul of humanity is at stake one must, if necessary, also stoop to the use of clichés. I call a spade a spade and I am not ashamed of it.

We are neglecting the health, both physical and moral, of the nation. We are lagging in vital areas of research that the possibilities indicate could in time turn this world into a virtual heaven on earth or if misused, a hell. We are neglecting the arts, without which civilizations come and go without seeming to have ever existed. Worst of all, we are neglecting what should be the bottom line dignity of our citizens. Below this line you not only fail to have democracy, but the worst possible despotism becomes a real alternative.

The bottom line of democracy should be full employment by either private industry or government for all that are willing and able to work or comparable compensation for not working: compensation that in no way should be considered welfare. Democracy should not be a safety net to catch human refuse, but should instead be a bottom line of equality and prosperity below which there is nothing but desperation (quiet or otherwise), economic slavery and despotism (benign or otherwise). Free education should be available to train people in these fast-changing times for any job for which they have aptitude. Healthcare for major illnesses should be free to all. For those in the arts or other occupations that embellish a society, but for which the necessary skills take years to develop fully, there should be a stipend income equal to that paid to people who cannot find jobs. This indeed, by our present standards, sounds utopian, but anything else is not democracy (Equal opportunity as opposed to absolute equality) and should be called by its proper name. (The United States is a republic) Democracy should be utopianesque with a goal of becoming utopia. (Utopia meaning the perfect state as opposed to the original meaning of the word, which was "nowhere". Democracy today is the same as the original definition of utopia) It is economic, if not political despotism to limit people options the way they are now limited in America and elsewhere. The bottom line must include complete freedom of choice as to how, where and what you want to do for a living. In America, you have unlimited free choice, but most of the good choices are out of reach for the average person. For many, there are no jobs at all, let alone one that offers personal fulfillment. Also, there is practically no retraining of people for jobs that are available for people who have the right qualifications, but cannot afford to retrain, unless, as is often not the case, job aspirants can afford the necessary training themselves. One thing truly instant in America is poverty, particularly if you lose your job. Thus, in the richest nation that has ever existed, you have a unique spectacle for all the world to see; able-bodied humanity by the millions, living in a never never land of underemployment, virtually next door to over a million millionaires and hundreds of billionaires.

The ideal democracy, which is the only real democracy, would be a country where government combined freedom of personal choice and material security as guarantees of birthright. Such a government would probably have to be a synthesis of the best attributes of capitalism and socialism, a synthesis capable of creating enough wealth to make everyone moderately well to do. We must, as we have always had the capacity to do, if we really wanted to, eliminate the poor by making everyone decently rich. Corporations + government = pseudo democratic fascism. Socialism + capitalism + citizen government supremacy = real democracy.

Chapter 4.

Economic Despotism

Economic despotism is, as you might guess, the opposite of economic democracy. And I do not think there is any in-between to make compromises about. Economic democracy means the economic-political system of a country is run for the benefit of the people, all the people, not just a majority of the powerful and beautiful in the prime of life or a minority of the rich and prestigious. If this is the case, how does America stack up to this definition of democracy?

America's official spin machine through several presidential administrations has been relentlessly harping to the world that free enterprise capitalism of the American type and democracy are inseparably synonymous. The message clearly implied is that one cannot exist without the other. That China is disproving this big lie fiction might be the understatement of all time. China is now decentralizing its economic system into an American style free enterprise system, but it is still a communist political despotism. Is America an economic despotism? By the above definition of democracy, the answer has to be yes. It is oligarchic corporatism that dominates the so-called democratic system in America and not the other way around. This is not free enterprise. One thing you can be sure of. The corporate boards that dominate America are concerned for their bottom lines first and the benefit to the American people not at all. It is socialized corporatism. This is why democracy in America is pseudo-democracy.

In America and most of the world today, what we call a countries economy is a conglomeration of small businesses and huge corporations that are frequently multi-national in the scope of their operations. Government spending is also a huge factor in the economy. Many of these corporations have assets exceeding those of many of the worlds countries. The only flag these companies hold exclusive allegiance to is the one with money on it. When they can, which is often the case, they act in many ways like the sovereign powers of money they are.

Those operating in the United States reserve the right to export our economy overseas when it is to their advantage. The Ford Motor Company at one time unabashedly threatened automobile workers with the loss of jobs to foreign countries if domestic wage demands were not reduced. They threatened to buy more parts from partially owned subsidiaries in Japan and elsewhere. And this arrogance was in full view of the fact that their own policies of exporting capital and technology was largely the cause of their predicament. At the same time that the company was using the threat of foreign competition against its workers, the chairman of the board of the company was crying like a voice in the wilderness about the unfair competition from Japan, competition his company was partially responsible for creating. The funny thing about this seeming contradiction of principles is that, even though the Chairman of the Ford Motor Company sounded like he was crying wolf, he was exactly correct. Now Ford's dire threats seem to be coming true, but in an ironic way. Ford is massively downsizing again in 2006. Soon they will probably be gone in spite of protests to the contrary by top management. American companies just cannot seem to compete with the imports even if the imports are made in America like Toyota and others. Or made by their overseas subsidiaries. Irrespective of who started the competitive bloodbath causing this economic meltdown, the downsizing and disappearance of so many traditional American companies that provided a secure life to so many American workers for so long is a grave threat to many of the things Americans have come to believe is a graven in stone birthright.

How America is to survive competition for a limited world market without destroying the world market we intentionally created is the big economic puzzle of the century? One thing we can be certain of at this point. There is no graven in stone economic security under the present world economic system. Competition is king and the economic winners are going to be those countries and companies that have the competitive edge.

Japan's Toyota Motors is projected number two in domestic American car sales in 2006 to General Motors by only a small margin and Ford is a distant third. What is even more shocking, GM appears on the brink of a complete meltdown. This is globalization at work. There are impressive claims that all this is beneficial. But to whom? We are told that half the world's population now is prospering because of a global market. Inflation is low, recessions are fewer and not as deep the mantra goes. One can only wonder at how all this is going to play out. One thing is a certainty. When all our high paying American jobs are gone and we are all pulling rickshaws for a living, we will be able to compete in the global market. That is, if we haven't auto-genocided ourselves out of existence first. I may be mistaken, but weren't we doing pretty well before globalization?

These three global companies are some of the biggest "multis".

Contrary to popular belief, multi-national corporations such as these operate, not according to the principle tenet of free enterprise, a market based on the law of supply and demand, but according to the main principle of a socialist state - a planned economy. Under a planned economy concept of pricing, the free enterprise concept, that the price of a product is based on the market value determined by the law of supply and demand, is obsolete with a few exceptions. Because it takes so many years to implement any economic plan, a company or state must know from the conception of any product line how many of each unit must be sold and what to charge for the finished product in order to make a profit. And they know these figures; because I have heard the head of GM publicly state this fact. This is not market capitalism. It is planned socialist economics. Unfortunately American politicians have never come to grip with this reality. Consequently no appropriate adjustments to our economic considerations have been made. This is one of the main reasons many American companies have lost their competitive edge. Our core economic model is out of sync with the reality of modern economics. Contrary to what we are constantly being told, we are not operating under a world market economic system, but instead, a world of competing socialist planned corporate economies. A contorted economic paradigm is what characterized the Soviet empire and caused the collapse of the Soviet Union and its empire. The Soviet economic model was really state corporatism organized to make a profit for the state, just as large free market corporations are small socialist states in the economic way they are organized to make a profit. What the Soviets didn't realize is that state corporations can also have losses and go belly up if they are managed incompetently, taking the state with them. The Soviet socialist corporation made one big mistake. It failed to compete on a world scale or to obey the laws of competitiveness that are based on profit and loss. Consequently it had bigger and bigger losses until it economically imploded. Corporations that do not compete on a world scale are blindsided to economic reality and cannot control their profit and losses, even if they are a monopoly. Because of this, the Soviet corporate state was insufferably incompetent to operate efficiently or profitably. Their products were of undesirable quality and the whole system of distribution was a disaster. What really bankrupted the Soviet system was not competition with America in arms production, as much as it was a failure to cooperate with other corporations in competition for world markets that would have been a reality check for them. This cooperation, as seen by China's example, is crucial in order to become competitive in the world market. World-class economies must be integrated fully into all aspects of worldwide trade from financing to distribution. Today, the multi-national corporation owns the world and even if identified with a particular national sovereignty, it is still beholden only to its own agenda that encompasses the whole world. You only have to look at the recent capitulation of American information companies to China's censorship laws, repugnant to Americans, to see that this is true. America survived the arms race competition by doing just the opposite of the Soviet Union. It capitulated to the multi-national model by allowing its corporations to promote the concept of free trade that expanded its business acumen around the world. This meant dismantling our great tariff wall and sharing our economy in ways that had never been done before. This greater economic base is what allowed America to survive the expensive competition of the arms race and remain a viable and flourishing nation. There are a number of crucial advantages to this competitive cooperation. There is a reality check that prevents the inevitability of incompetent management, such as that of the Soviet Union from becoming terminally out of touch with market reality. Unacceptable losses compared to competitors will cause the replacement of such incompetent management in an attempt to re-sync with acceptable norms. This cooperation is best exemplified in the financial sphere. Chinese companies can readily obtain financing in the American capital markets at the same time that China is financing much of America's trade/budgetary debt by investing in hundreds of billions of dollars of our debt. While nominally, America and China are supposed to have opposing economic systems hostile to one another, the truth is they don't. The hostility is all macho political posturing over nationalistic sensitivities. Even though multis out of necessity price their products without regard to a market price as socialist monopolies do, there is still an element of risk, because they must compete with other multis. The ones therefore that will have the competitive edge will be the ones that, all things considered, will have the most desirable product, price often being the most important factor. These multi-national companies that are the dominant world economic model today must, then compete with each other when, paradoxically, they must plan their operations like monopolies. Therefore, what has occurred in the world is a completely new economic order that no one has been willing to acknowledge exists, because monopoly is a bad word and socialist monopoly is even worse. The Japanese were capitalizing for years on the failure of the rest of the world to come to grips with this reality. They were the only country that geared up to deal effectively with worldwide socialist monopoly competition.

These multi mini-socialist states that call themselves corporations claim to be operating within the framework rules of a free enterprise market system. They are really operating independently of this market economy as a part of a duel economic system that is one part a market driven supply and demand free enterprise system and one part a socialist planned economy. The huge socialistically planned corporations are clearly the dominant part of this duel economic system. Their mistakes, vision or lack of vision and the competitiveness made possible by cooperation or lack of cooperation between themselves, government, labor and foreign competitors is directly responsible for the economic health or sickness of modern nations. To put it bluntly, the economic health of modern nations is directly related to the business acumen of its transnationals and their ability to compete for foreign and local markets.

The business acumen of many large American corporations is in question today, because there have been many American losers in the competitive race between American multis and foreign multis. Therefore, the job creating responsibility of large American corporations is shifting from large to small corporations and individual proprietorships. Some of the unemployment caused by replaced large American corporations is being taken up by foreign owned competitors that replace them. It remains to be seen if this will be a satisfactory job creating strategy.

It is said that large companies are the last to exploit breakthrough technology. True or not, and this is not always true except as a generalization, America is lagging behind others who do exploit our technology. I don't think this is really the main problem. As an example of who uses competitive tech, the latest robotics technology is being used by American automakers to reduce the cost of making cars. This is an attempt to be competitive with the Japanese and now the Koreans and soon China. However, the American companies are still losing market share and now the big auto companies are blaming the baggage of pensions for their troubles. The burden of pensions is being shifted into 401K savings plans where most of the money will be invested in the stock market. This is a double plus for the corporations. Pensions will soon be a thing of the past, as much as the carrier pidgin. A cataclysmic economic metamorphosis seems to be looming on the horizon, but the government goes blissfully on its unconcerned way. It now appears that the American traditional automobile companies will go the way of the consumer electronics and other industries. However, it is significant that auto companies are being replaced by other mostly foreign owned companies building their own plants on American soil. The question is then, are we losing market share that will result in a job depression or just changing ownership and names of companies. In the auto industry at least, the answer seems to be the latter.

It is left for smaller companies, whose executives have often gained management expertise or made new discoveries while working for the multies or universities, to exploit breakthrough technology. Venture capitol is readily available to certain kinds of new businesses who have a desirable business plan, although this doesn't always prevent the leakage of new tech overseas in cases where the inventor prefers to sell his invention to the highest bidder. The biggest problem with our economy relying on foreign industry to supply manufactured goods is that the more the American economy is hollowed out by the loss of a manufacturing infrastructure, the less there will be engineers and researchers working to make new discoveries that will result in new industries. This becomes a bigger and bigger problem as less and less students go into fields in which jobs may no longer be available. Many American citizens are now working overseas, even in India as interns, in order to be able to work in fields of their training in which jobs are not available in the U.S. Foreigners who were imported to the U.S. by American companies are now running much of American high tech to make up for the slack of available qualified talent. The question seems to be not so much the economic fallout damage winners cause to losers between competing multies, as it is, are the winners satisfactory replacements for the losers?

America has become a conglomerate of many big corporations with one subsidiary, the government. There should be a separation of business and state in the United States based on the same principle as that which justifies separation of church and state. The government cannot serve the people fairly if it is serving other competing masters for its favors at the same time. The government is the only effective power that can represent the people's rights because most individual people do not have the economic clout necessary to sway the government by hiring lobbyists the way corporations can afford to.

However, any country that wants to have a world-class economy must have business entities powerful enough to effectively compete around the world. Small countries or countries that do not wish to compete must find other ways to create a viable local economy. Whatever way that is, they cannot depend on the efficacy of the so-called law of comparative advantage for help, because this is a complete farce. There is no such thing, as is claimed, that every country possesses a comparative advantage exclusivity of some job type and everyone knows it except it seems people who teach it as a law in university economic courses. (Unless you live on an island that is a big pile of guano) It is a cruel hoax at this point to perpetuate this myth, but it is perpetuated in spite of this. There needs to be another solution for smaller countries with no comparative advantage and no multi-national corporations. My solution for all countries big and small is a plan called Parity Economics. This will be elaborated on in a succeeding chapter.

The correct legal perspective concerning a corporation's relationship to governments is that it is a licensed entity of a sovereign state granted the privilege of conducting business as long as it obeys the laws of that sovereign state. It is a privilege, much like a driver's license. The corporation is a licensed independent entity of the state and the state is an agent of the people, not the other way around, as it now often seems to be the case. However, in a bizarre role reversal, it is not uncommon in the American congress, on issues affecting them that corporate lobbyists sometimes write the laws that are often passed by legislators who don't bother to even read them. This is democracy? I don't think so. I think this describes oligarchy, not democracy. The influence that corporations have purchased through the use of lobbyists and campaign contributions to the representatives of the people has overwhelmed the political system. We cannot allow the government to be acting as an agent for corporations and expect the people's rights to be protected. At present, the corporations are free to prey on the people practically at will and say, in the words of General Mobuto of Zaire, "What is good for me is good for the country". We think the country would be a lot better served if corporations were made responsible in many areas, including: creating permanent security for their employees, contributing a fair share to the culture of the country, gracefully obeying the environmental, pollution, drug, food and other laws - instead of trying to circumvent these laws as they now do because they have so much influence. In general these dominant giants should attempt to be benevolent instead of exploitative of a country and its people. It is time for corporations to stop killing the goose that lays the golden egg or they will self-destruct when people are so impoverished they are unable to balance the production of these corporations with their ability to consume that production, causing an economic train wreck. Contrary to this thought, corporations, not satisfied with merely having the American government in their back pockets to do every outrageous thing they want, they are importing high-end tech workers we don't need, who will take less pay than available American workers. They are also outsourcing white-collar jobs by the thousand that can be done and are needed by American workers. They are now, through their lobbyist bribed so-called representatives of the people, making the poorest segment of the American population pay for their bought administration's culpable stupidity and corrupt rush to war.

This is seen to be especially true in the Bush 2 administration through which, having feared the erosion of their power, they have asserted themselves and are crudely rolling back virtually every democratic advance that has been made in recent years to inhibit their freewheeling lack of responsibility toward the country as a whole. It is as if in a single moment, all the hard won battles in the war to more intelligently utilize our resources have been lost to the despots of greed. Everything that is today being done by the Republican administration in the economic sphere revolves around making things easier for the corporation, because the corporation and other forms of big business are thought to be our main economic salvation, especially for them. We agree that big business is crucial to economic well-being, but disagree vehemently with the present methods being used to help it, methods which are detrimental to the people and the planet. It is claimed that our economy is booming at the moment even though I believe in many ways it is seriously foundering. Booming compared to what is the real question. We are living a hollowed out economy producing inferior jobs compared to not many years ago. Higher corporate profits and the advancing stock market should not be the main yardstick for how well the economy is performing. Ruining the quality of life to boost the bottom line of corporations is not a good choice for people. Unfortunately, we are certain that the present course is not only leading to the ruination of the quality of life but will lead to eventual economic ruin of the country as well. The Bureau of Labor Statistics shows that high-end jobs are being replaced with low-end jobs. If you are an engineer, you better get training to be a bartender. This is due to government policies virtually dictated by corporations. The administration knows it and is spinning the truth to make it seem that there is no job problem. It seems that this country is hell bent on self-destruction.

After we feel we have adequately diagnosed the disease, we hope to offer some alternative solutions to the economic problem that will make possible a united effort by all segments of society to save our society from having to choose between quality of life disaster on the one hand and catastrophic economic degeneration on the other hand. If we cannot have an economy that provides good jobs, a healthy environment and a happy educated healthy society all at the same time we are cheating ourselves and making grave mistakes somewhere.

Business alone is not responsible for economic despotism and blindness. Government shares a great deal of that responsibility.

However, it is a thesis of this book that government regulation has been biased in favor of big business because big business has the most influence with government, no matter what party is in power. It is not the idea here to be a prophet of doom, but to set the stage, by a certain amount judicious demolition for the possibility of great renovation. And it's not all fertilizer we hope.

While we should strive for more economic democracy, by making possible the resurgence of the great individualist entrepreneur who has been shunted aside by giant global corporations, I think the giant corporation is a necessity and should not be hounded and over regulated just because of its size. Bureaucracies that form an economic plan that takes years to implement are necessary in a world of billions of people, and where there is competition between countries for a huge world market. The government's relationship to business should be like a Shepard tending its flock. But the Shepard should understand that its employer is the people, and not the corporation. We agree that the way should be made as easy as possible for corporations to succeed, but not at the expense of quality democracy or allowing corporate economic despotism, such as is now the case. While the great corporations serve a useful purpose, they are not the only or even the main avenue of job formation in America at present. Small businesses have a great role to play and the way should be opened for these and all business individualists to reemerge in every area of business. Much that is now closed to entrepreneurs because the playing field is uneven and stacked against them by the current unfair world economic system should be once again made viable to all business. In another succeeding chapter, we will offer a solution to this problem of leveling the playing field called Parity Economics.

Chapter 5.

The Pseudo Democracies

It is the indictment of this book that the fruits of the labor of the common man are being stolen or squandered by governments of all kinds, the world over: democracies as well as non-democracies. The leaders of the world do not have a clue, let alone a vision, of what the future must be like if man is to even survive, let alone evolve into space age man. It is the mission of this book to envision what life can be like and what all of us together, the common men and women can do to force our leaders to make the changes necessary to bring about a new kind of people oriented world.

Man has not even begun to learn how to truly democratize the two things most important to him - his economy and his personal freedom. I think Eric Fromm was quite right when he suggested the idea that all societies are insane. And most of us, being products of the values and illusions of the societies in which we live are, consequently, neurotically out of touch with reality to a dangerous degree. We should strive, then, to resolve our personal conflicts - not by seeking help from those who are swamped in a sea of confusion, but by helping to create a sane society. Much of our finest literature reflects the hypocrisy rampant in Western Civilization. The holocaust of World War II reflected this moral degeneration of Western man better than any words. When brotherly love is missing from life, the meaning of life becomes hate. Western man, in spite of all superficial piety, is dominated by the values of a predatory animal. There are few exceptions to this rule. The United States has the most predatory ideology in the world and, consequently, as a result, it has by far the most violent crime rate. Some of our most respected recent films reflect disillusionment with the American dream and validly question whether it is ever going to be more than a dream for many people. This is a judgment that the moral criterion of this book has indorsed. We are not truly a democracy if, as has always been the case, a segment of our population is denied justice. Mankind has one collective choice. To create heaven or hell.

Choosing a politician in America is similar to taking a walk on the beach looking for nirvana in the form of the perfect beauty to seduce. We wallow about in the sand in hopes of finding the ideal lover of our dreams: the one who will fulfill all our fantasies. It is a gullible fantasy to think this will succeed with politicians, even though you might get lucky at the beach. There is just no way, without being patronizing, of describing America's choice of politicians, except gullible. I am sure our people are no more gullible than people in other countries, but we may be more vulnerable to deceit due to the way we run our elections. The human race has an entire history of gullibility about leaders, which is one of the reasons man has always been an easy dupe of his rulers. Of course the power of rhetoric is such that clever minds are sometimes able to fool even the best-educated constituency. This is why we have recall laws. Unfortunately the winner of a recall may be worse than the pol that was replaced. We did it in California, but many of us who favor the poor now regret our vote. Arnold has shown amazing political courage and aplomb considering his background, but he is still a Republican. Even so, his spunk makes him hard to dislike even as he attempts to wreck havoc on settled democratic issues, such as a union's right to use their member's dues to back candidates of their choice. His attempt to overturn by initiative this right would have set a dangerous precedent for the country, if successful. The following is a little but important digression, but I think people should know about this. The initiative movement started in California as a grass roots volunteer movement that has had some great successes. Initiatives are direct democracy whereby anyone who can collect enough signatures on a petition can have it put on the ballad and voted on. To counter these direct democracy initiatives, politicians, corporations and others have jumped on the initiative bandwagon with their money and now pay people to get signatures on initiatives that benefit their interests. There is nothing wrong with this except the ethics of the duplicity they practice to get people to sign up. The latest and greatest way they use to trick people to sign, besides the tricky way petition synopses are worded, is to hand people six initiatives at the same time, most of which are innocuously people friendly and ask them to sign, all of them. The first few are obviously people friendly. Among the pile is one or two that most people are opposed too, usually placed toward the end. Most people read one or two that sound good and not wanting to take a lot more time reading synopses just sign the rest, assuming they too are innocuously friendly. They are doing this right now with the to build or not to build a LNG terminal at Long Beach harbor that most people don't want. Instead of building this 22 miles off shore, as one company wants to do, they want to put it right at a terminal on land near existing oil refineries. If it blows it takes out everything within a seven-mile radius, which will include miles of refineries and fuel storage adjacent to the terminal. It will be worse than an A-bomb. Seven miles is most of Long Beach. They have been doing everything, including constant direct mail; TV PR advertising, public meetings and you name it to convince the public to go for the land terminal. These are the kind of horrendous corporate activities contemptuous of public safety, totally unnecessary, since they have a viable alternative, which should be penalized. This attitude makes one really want to hate corporations.

If you do not have real democracy encompassing both economic and political individual rights, democracy is just an empty word. One without the other leads to a pseudo everything government. That is just what we have in the United States. You cannot separate the two if you want real democracy. It seems that a lot of people do not understand this. The denial of opportunity rights to part of the population is an insidious denial of democracy. This has the effect of leaving the individual in a "divide and conquer" state of helplessness in the face of the powerful and rich. The U.S. congress endorsed shafting the most needy part of the people again on 12/21/05 by cutting programs for the poor by forty billion. It was passed by a tie-breaking vote of the vice president. This sends the message, unlimited money for stupidly run wars and cuts for the poor to pay for them. It makes you sick at your stomach. This kind of scandalous policy making is a terrible blot on the name of democracy and an example that will not go unnoticed by the rest of the world we are always bragging to about what a great capitalist democracy we have. We must think we are still living in the Stone Age when drums and smoke signals transmitted information. Even drum communication would not hide the fact that the masters of greed are on the throne of what is laughingly called capitalist democracy.

This government under W., that claims a conservative agenda, is doing the same thing in all areas of services to people, including military veterans. For or against wars, we feel strongly that those who have served their country deserve to be given special treatment in health care, education and other essentials. This is sometimes but not always the case and quality health care for veterans is being constantly whittled away by a little cut here and a little cut there. The current administration is a bottomless well of shamelessness.

The recent prescription drug controversy was another shameless example of corporate dictatorship in action. The whole act was cleverly written by the drug companies to sell drug plans to people who don't need plans. The media has never figured this out. All they talked about was plans and confused seniors. The word plan never needed to be mentioned. The whole thing was really simple. If you had an HMO, you didn't have to sign up for anything. If you didn't have an HMO or want one, you also didn't have to sign up for anything. Everything was done by phone. No one had to sign up for any drug plan or anything else. The catch was, the HMO's you were assigned by Social Security insisted when you called them that you needed a plan that had a premium. They dummied up and waited for the suckers to sign up for a plan. It was a form of bait and switch. Millions of people are no doubt now paying for drug plans they don't need. This was the intention of the whole scam. This confusion was intentional to fool the uninformed and it worked with the full complicity of the government and the stupidity of the media. Those under the poverty line are entitled to a special category called "extra help" by social security that entitles them to even lower drug prices. At the beginning, it was almost impossible to get through to Social Security and obtain the "extra help" designation. You had to request of Social Security that you be so designated on their computers or the HMO's claimed not to know anything about it. "Everybody needs a plan" was their mantra. The clerks at social security that answered the phones had not been trained about it and would drop you unless you got hold of a supervisor and requested you be stipulated "extra help" on the computers. They knew, but not the phone clerks that had to do the work. By the time the clerks had the right answers, the panic was on.

The U.S. under Carter began a policy that stood for reforms that would better the lot of poor farmers in the third world. This policy, which apparently is still in effect in 2006, recently cost the lives of two American workers in San Salvador. Ironically, we seem to hypocritically stand for the antithesis of land reform as a national policy, as opposed to an international policy. There is a flagrant violation of the law going on in California in areas of publicly funded water reclamation where the size of holdings are stipulated by law to try to favor small farmers. Large landholders, however, have refused to give up their oversized holding's rights, because these holdings have increased so dramatically in value. Land and water reform be damned. So therefore, American democracy is not only pseudo but hypocritical in some instances.

Jimmy Carter, a very unpopular president because of his

disastrous handling of the Iran hostage crises, initiated a high-minded moral policy toward the rest of the world that is probably the best instance of an American policy that was not tarnished by a self-serving ulterior motive since the Marshall Plan. The Iranian religious despots and fanatics successful revolution is one of the best examples of the desperation of people of the third world to find an antidote for the economic colonialism of the superpowers that discredited both Democracy and Soviet Communism. This, as ludicrous as it seems, may in fact be the main motive behind the terrorist war we are now fighting and losing. It is perceived that the oil money is going to the elite and America is thought to be somehow responsible because the price of oil is too low. (At least before its recent rise, $75 per barrel 4/21/06) Carter's anecdote to the moral poison labeling of America as the great Satan was the articulation of the human rights problem, one of the missing links in world sanity. This probably made more genuine friends for America among the world's intellectual elite community than all the money we have ever spent on foreign aid put together. Unfortunately, because of the P.R. mistakes made under the pressure of the war on terror, we have regressed in the eyes of the world, to a position of moral poison personified. (I think the current president of Iran's madman rhetoric is calculated to cause enough controversy to run up oil prices. No wonder he is popular with Russia, one of the world's leading oil producers. Of course, we have taken the bate, as have the Israelis)

Reagan quite correctly perceived that the USSR's Achilles heel was the awareness of people around the world, in this age of instant communications, that the communist's fundamental doctrine of material equality was a false promise made at the sacrifice of personal freedom. Everyone in the world today, who is not, still living in a bubble, knows that the dictatorship of the proletariat is just plain dictatorship. What saved the United States from a Communist world order more than anything else may not have been all the arms we produced and money we spent, but the perception by people everywhere that Communism equals an extremely dangerous way to solve problems. Communism is like the female black widow spider that eats its mate after being inseminated.

The Chinese, out of desperation to change a corrupt incompetent Nationalist government, took the path of communism as an alternative to the famine and other chaotic conditions that had always existed under capitalism and monarchy in China. It seems that capitalism has a progressively more difficult time as the size of a population grows. I think this seeming exponential growth of problems in relation to growth of population size is due to the inherently inhumane nature of unbridled capitalism that considers itself synonymous with democracy. It tends to let problems get out of hand before it attempts to remedy the situation. This may be because the capitalist system by its nature prefers a divide and conquer uncoordinated organization of society that encourages disunity and disorganization, except in the case of the exploiters that can take advantage of such conditions. Today, these culprits mainly are corporations that have literally pulled all the democratic stops out. (A corporation is a well-organized mini-state within a state that because of its economic clout becomes the real government) We think there is some law of organizations, obvious to all but the obfuscators, that says that governments require growing in size, in direct proportion to the size of the governing responsibilities. This is no different than the way corporations and other large organizations have to increase in size as the workload increases. This flies directly contrary to the divide and conquer mantra of smaller government is better government that has been drummed into us by the GOP conservative P.R. spin machine. The conservative/radical mantra of smaller government is just more senseless dishonest rhetoric by dishonest politicians and bought media intent on weakening government for their own nefarious purposes, mostly excessive corporate profit. You can't just proclaim smaller government is better and make it smaller. It has to be the right size to do the job. What they really mean is make government so weak it has no power to curb corporate excesses. Smaller government also makes possible smaller corporate bureaucracy to deal with its government restrictions and other problems. Even Bush has found big government is a necessity of big population and has wisely forfeited on the smaller is better mantra in spite of the venom it has evoked from fellow conservatives. This shows, God help us, he is smarter or more honest than a lot of his followers. It also is soon going to be discovered that we are no longer a capitalist democracy. We have merged with socialism and there is no turning back.

The Chinese have clearly become disillusioned with the limitations of communist economics and are attempting at present to have a capitalist economic system and communist political system side by side. They are trying to find a way of incorporating the best elements of socialism and capitalism in order to have, if possible, the better of both worlds. So far, they are succeeding very well economically. They are not having much luck changing their communist political image from that of a dictatorship to that of a democracy, however. Let us hope they change more than just the image if they ever have elections and decide to declare themselves a democracy. They have rewritten their constitution with a view towards making it legal to have a mixed communist-capitalist political-economic system. They have done this in a draconian joke of a way by giving the workers the right to find their own jobs. Like they are doing them a favor! Of course this means the government is no longer responsible for employing everyone as it was before. This frees the government to dispose of obsolete money losing industry and compete in the world economy on an equal footing with other capitalist countries. It seems then China has become a socialist country in name only. A system that is not responsible for creating full employment should not claim to be a socialist country. This policy is working very well for China in the economic sphere and its economy is booming for those that have taken the capitalist road. In the social sphere, they are having the same kind of problems now, as we have in the capitalist world. Unemployment that used to be forbidden now exists big time; huge environmental problems - especially pollution, health, income disparity and other problems are causing widespread unrest in much of the country. This is a world shaking breakthrough experiment in socio-economic-political engineering, but has been ignored in this sense by the inept Western media. The prospect of a communist country breaking all the economic stereotypes we have been led to believe are the necessary concomitants of a communist system is truly earth shattering. It is fast looking like the twenty-first century is going to be the Chinese century economically. Until the revolution.

I wonder whether our brilliant leaders have not destined America to the status of a "have not" third world nation. The United States has chosen to have an almost one-sided free trade policy with many of the countries of the world. Unfortunately, this perhaps wise survival tactic has never been corrected. This has given many other countries of the world a chance, by economic cooperation with American companies and development of their own multi-national corporations, a chance to have flourishing capitalist or in some cases capitalist-socialist economies. We originally promulgated this magnanimous policy out of politically expedient self-interest because we did not want to end up like the old Lone Ranger joke, with only one friend and surrounded by hostile socialist Indians. The hypothetical punch line? The British deserted us when labor lost. The only embarrassing paradoxical problem is that, while trying to buy friends, we have bought deadly economic enemies. Because we have shared the wealth to a far greater degree than we ever intended, we might no longer be able to comfortably do everything we have been doing in the recent past at home and abroad. This includes: financing a social safety net security at home, providing a military umbrella police force for the entire world, staying ahead in the space race, and solving a whole host of problems for the whole world.

But of more far reaching significance is whether we are in danger of becoming a second rate economic power. Our economy, while still powerful, is only a fragment of what it should be. And that is really the overriding problem. The American population has been hyped into auto-genocidal birth control because of the failure of the economy to expand fast enough. Except for the de-industrialization that is eliminating our entire manufacturing base, we would have millions more jobs and millions more indigenous Americans than we have now, if people had well paying secure jobs to support bigger families. As it is, we cannot provide jobs for thousands of unemployed professionals who are the engines of economic expansion, and millions of others are either unemployed or working at inappropriate, underpaid survival jobs. Having hyped the American people on birth control that has made possible the auto-genocide of our people, and having allowed our economy to falter and flee abroad, and having spent our surplus and gone into unbelievable debt to build an unmatchable military to fight endless wars, we are staring moral, physical and financial bankruptcy right in the face. This has provided a protective umbrella not only for us, but also for our economic rivals that are taking our jobs. You would think that the minimum the masters of our fate would do to reward this sacrifice is reward the people of America with a super-secure life of full employment. Instead, job security is dead, social security is in intensive care and we have a morale problem of truly Herculean proportions in this country. Between the high cost of living and insecurity many people, who have an option because of ubiquitous birth control devices, are barely willing and able to reproduce themselves. At the same time, the desperate third world proliferates out of control and clambers to get in our gates. The difficulty of surviving the economic pressure of America is such that people are increasingly turning to self destructively reprehensible lifestyles instead of a healthy family life. The resulting vacuum is being filled by a massive legal and illegal immigration that threatens to destroy traditional American culture.

In an economic system such as Americas, that turns a cold shoulder to anyone who does not at all times have a high paying job, the high cost of living sentences those who dare stray away from the main stream to almost immediate poverty from which it is almost as difficult to escape as a maximum-security prison. People's jobs are in no way secure in America, the land of the free. If you do not have a continuous, and what is considered "good" employment record, even education and experience will not do you much good when you try to get a job. After the age of forty, even with a good employment record and the best of educations, you are in grave danger of losing your job to someone younger who does not care that the same thing might be happening to him or her in a few years. Good luck when your old worn-out worker of forty or so goes to get another comparable job. This of course applies to the non-unionized white collar worker who considers himself part of the establishment. It even applies to those with the best education and skills. There is no safe-haven anymore for a job in private enterprise that is secure for life. We have a terrible morale problem in the United States because of the star system winner take all way of doing things that rewards people as take all winners and losers take none. This causes a great conflict of values in a society that professes to be based on sane Judeo-Christian values of love and sharing, but is really pervasively hypocritically absurd.

Some of the things that reflect the low morale of Americans are: the worst voter turnouts for elections of any country in the world, a low birthrate except for unsuspecting immigrants whose medical costs are picked up by the taxpayers, high violent crime rates, a high suicide rate, and pervasive drug and alcohol abuse and addiction. There are subtler manifestations of poor morale, such as the poor attitude people have towards their fellow human beings in trouble. Instead of helping, we turn our backs.

The pseudo democracies claim to be interested in the greatest good for the greatest number. The opposite is patently true. If life were truly democratic, it would become possible for people to act with more initiative to solve their problems. Every entity, whether the entity is one individual or a massive corporation, needs financing from time to time. Only the large corporation can obtain financing when it needs it, because it has the whole system at its beck and call. People do not.

Therefore, most people in capitalist countries cannot act as individualists because they cannot always finance education, homes and businesses when they need to. Now, with inflation creeping back, interest rates going up and the big bucks necessary to do anything, the average person is lucky to survive, let alone be able to function as an individualist. People today, really do not have much of a chance to be individualists and compete in a capitalist economy, because big government and big business, which is essentially the same thing, are both working together to exploit the little people. The business of America, should not be just business. Rich countries should lead the way in support of the arts, sciences and other non-commercial disciplines, simply because they have the most money and it takes surplus to make these, the highest of all human activities, take root and flower. In this country we have done nothing comparable to our gross national product to support the liberal arts. And this amount is being shrunk currently. What do we cherish most in history, the art and philosophy of ancient Athens or the military expertise of the Spartans? Our entire civilization today is built on the building blocks of Athens that started almost three thousand years ago. The future will be looking at what we do or do not do now to make a contribution to world culture. The prognosis, I'm afraid is not very good. This comes of putting rednecks and other ignoramuses in charge of the purse strings. Whatever man and woman's purpose on this earth is, it is not to vegetate. Sparta is gone and all but forgotten, while Athens is still vibrantly alive in our culture after thousands of years. In a thousand years are we going to be looked upon as heirs of Athens or Sparta? Maybe we should rename our most popular brand of condoms Athens instead of Trojans to remind us of whose heritage we value the most.

If you are not swimming in the main stream in America, you are out there swimming in deadly shark-infested waters. By representing corporate interests in a disproportionate way, government has usurped the power from the people, allowing them to be divided and conquered. We have allowed ourselves to be fooled and misled by fools, because we have permitted a foolish political system that does not protect us from the predators. We must give the power back to ourselves by renewing and improving our democratic principles.

Chapter 6.

Parity Economics

Man is on the threshold of a new age. Nothing could better exemplify the radical changes in lifestyle this new age is going to bring about than robotics. Robots are already "on line" in factories around the world in what could be called foreboding numbers. Contrary to what management is telling workers who fear for their jobs, most labor now performed by workers will, within the next fifty years, be performed by robots.

Robots are a significant factor in Japanese industry where they have no doubt played a significant role in the Japanese dominance of some important industries. In the automobile industry these humanoid machines work twenty-four hours a day, seven days a week, 365 days a year, never making a flaw, never complaining and never asking for a raise or fringe benefits. Hugh Hefner has had a robot servant serving drinks to his revelers for years. Millions of dollars a year in robots are being sold and manufactured in America by American companies, and this is just the beginning. Japan is setting the pace in this area, as in many others. These robots and other high tech tools that are probably going to replace all workers some day, are being built with technology that often is a spin-off of space/military technology paid for by American tax money. You can bet robots are going to replace regular workers, just as automation has. There is even a Santa Claus robot on the drawing boards that will be able to fly to another planet in the solar system, dig up natural resources, set up factories, procreate little self-replicating robot helpers, manufacture an unending stream of toys and send them back to earth by reindeer robots; all in an unending stream that will make everyday Christmas. We will literally be able to cannibalize our solar system so that junior can break it up the next day. The interplanetary environmentalists will no doubt put up a big squawk, but I feel confident junior will win the day. The only catch is, who is going to have a job and money to pay for these things except for porno magazine publishers?

This above anecdote may be a joke, but is government planning for the day in the future, less than fifty years from now, when this science fiction inevitability becomes real life? Of course not. In America, at least, those now in charge have convinced themselves and the country that the government doesn't have to plan for anything except the next war. It appears that we didn't do much planning for the latest war either. Or we used the wrong plan. The bad planning that was done and the results so far have implications of being the dumbest disaster in American history. Our entire army is pinned down in Iraq and appears to be helpless to defeat this enemy. It makes us appear to be a helpless stupid giant. This is psychologically and physically Vietnam all over again. All as a result of bad planning. This is not lost on our many enemies even if the stupid people now in charge of the white house are lost in a fog of denial. The people have to be protected from bad government such as this, but the question is how. By the time people wake up and change government under our current system, generations of damage will have been done.

Is it indeed possible that the chronic unemployment and underemployment we are suffering in developed countries is a natural concomitant of man's technological evolvement? Haven't we really reached a time when instead of lying to the public about how we are going to solve the unemployment problem, we should forth-rightly inform people that employment is going to be a privilege enjoyed by a smaller and smaller number of people we might conveniently call workaholics. We should, in view of ominous forecasts such as the above and chronic underemployment figures, at least consider this possibility and try to find alternative solutions. Instead, we let the sore fester and this canker besmirches the whole moral tone of our civilization.

If, in fact, we cannot possibly solve our employment problems, shouldn't we, instead of stigmatizing the unemployed as a bunch of lazy no-goods who are a burden on society, enshrine them as the wave of the future and use them as guinea pigs in the laboratory of life? These guinea pigs can help us explore the frontiers of what is soon to be a new lifestyle for all of us; a life of freedom to live the contemplative life or, better yet, freedom to live any life style we choose except that of an automaton robot. In other words, the reverse of the way things are now. Of course, we are talking about constructive life styles such as creative arts, playing games, craft pursuits, contemplative endeavors, semi-permanent school or anything that is work for man liberated from the factory. The important thing is that a person will choose work because it is work he wants to do, rather than work he does because the society needs that work to support an economy. For many people who seem to prefer being in a category with automatons, this presents a fearsome future, but according to some of the greatest thinkers who have ever lived, this is the dream life. It has been the theoretical dream life in the past, but it will be the mandatory life in the near future. Get ready to use your brains everybody. They were given to you according to my mom for some other reason than as hat racks. An idea such as this, as far removed as it is to present reality, is probably the stuff that pipe dreams are made of, even madness. I may be mad in several ways, but I did not just fall off a turnip truck. In the words of the immortal bard, you can pluck me but you can't shuck me without getting my corncob lit. Let's consider the big picture of the relationship of China to the United States. They in effect are paying the American worker right now not to work. How can this be? American workers would have to work much harder to buy the consumer goods they are getting from China at a much lower price than if they were made in America. At the same time, China is financing a large part of our astronomical national debt. Otherwise, we would have to pay much higher taxes, entailing working more hours to pay this tax. And only about 300 million of the 1.3 billion Chinese are performing this miracle. If instead of paying American workers to take their surplus production, they dumped it on their one billion subsistence farmers, Americans would have to go back to work again. But then, we would become competitors instead of customers. This will probably go down in history as the most unusual case of economics making strange bedfellows ever known. For sure, there are economic laws at work here that are valid somehow, but I don't think anyone knows what they are. Or they aren't telling. Whatever, they certainly seem to defy economic gravity.

Certainly one of the main reasons the human race is in the condition it is in (Bad in case you didn't know) is the mental myopia (Near-brainedness) that all politicians seem to be congenitally inflicted with. The Popes, representing the oldest continuous political organization in the world, have been suffering terminal myopia for five hundred years or so but somehow, seem to rally just in time to bless us once more with their infallible blunders that have done more to discredit the validity of Christ's ideas than all the atheists and anti-Christs put together. When there are more people inhabiting this planet per square inch than there are angels on the head of a pin they will no doubt come out for sensible birth control and take credit for saving the world. Politicians and priests are like torturers. The last one to turn the screw is hailed as a savior. At present, the Catholic hierarchy appears to be in a panic, as they and we should be because of the frightening array of dangerous challenges that face us. (A top cardinal recently came out for the use of condoms, which is a genuine miracle. He should be made an instant saint) The Pope because of the many frightening implications of current science is demonizing the whole of Western civilization as being Satanic. It is hard even for an agnostic to disagree. We are on the threshold of the empowerment of individuals to cheaply create and wield WMD's more fearsome than the worst there is today. Our very DNA is at risk. Name calling and taking the ostrich approach is not going to deal with this challenge. The genie is already out of the bottle. If responsible scientists are not allowed to deal with these problems, however, the irresponsible rogues will. Unfortunately our leaders can be counted on for little or no imagination; and in our time this could be suicidal for the human race. For example: how could our leaders, who are in a position of responsibility to know, not foresee or anticipate a problem as obvious as the energy crisis? Isn't that what we pay them for? We believe the truth is that legislators have no capacity to anticipate anything because they are so busy trying to survive in the here and now, thoughts of the future are just too much amperage for their little brains to cope with. We therefore need, in fact demand, a new Department of Anticipation that can fill this missing link in our government's knowledge base.

We cannot tackle problems we are hardly aware exist and certainly not in a coordinated planned way. There, I used that dirty word again. We do not now have such crucial information available. How can the government function rationally unless we allocate some of our best minds to deciding where we should concentrate our creative energies? Our very survival demands that we start using our God given reason instead of reading entrails ala the Romans.

The United States has become a Hollywood funny farm ala Eric Fromm. The stuff of insanity is that our government, which is supposed to represent the people, represents the exploiters of the people. Every day, before I sit down to work I read the newspaper or Internet about some new policy of the administration attributed in some way to our current leader. It has been almost like reading the book of revelation except the revelation is uniformly anti-poor people and anti-democratic. The Administration is trying in every way to back-pedal every democratic reform that has been made in this country. It is a case study in capitulation to the forces of predation. My purpose in this book is not so much to criticize the current administration, as it is to give an objective picture of the fallacies of the democratic system and offer some suggestions on how it can be improved. I have come to realize, in giving my full attention to the news, how and why it is so difficult for the average person to digest the full impact of government on their lives enough to prevent the erosion of their liberties. I'm not sure anybody can. Most people just do not have time or perhaps the education to meticulously study what the government is doing to them on a daily bases. How can they when there is so much information to deal with that even the senators and representatives claim they do not have enough time to read the bills before voting on them? It should be mandatory for them or their staffs to read these bills first before they vote. (A thousand page legal act would take me weeks or months to read and study, just the pork part probably) The rest of us are overwhelmed by just the feedback of material we get from the media. The devil and the pork are in the details unfortunately. Now they call it earmarks. The sums of earmarks have gone from thousands to millions to hundreds of millions in some cases such as that obscene bridge in Alaska and are given as a quid pro quo for voting on bills. What is truly shocking is that none of this makes much more than a ripple in the media. Here today gone tomorrow applies equally to the news and lives, but it is literally true of the news. The other side of the coin is, as I heard veteran reporter Helen Thomas ask, "Where are the people?" Obviously, the people are helpless and don't have a clue what to do. It's a stupid rhetorical question born of frustration to start with because that's why we elect people to congress. When the media and the congress have both capitulated to the corporate state the way they have, what are people supposed to do? There is really only one course left open to the people. Rioting in the streets, thank you Helen. And I don't think you are stupid. Just chagrined like the rest of us. If shocking exposés like you see on 60 minutes, the highest rated TV program hardly make a ripple, how can people make an impact?

In the United States we just do not have, and virtually never have had, except in time of war, a serious government. (Real wars as opposed to wars on poverty) There can never be a serious government in America until we have some law of truth that requires our leaders to back up their high-blown rhetoric and lavish promises with action; action that must be continued from one generation of leaders to the next. We find ourselves; at least I find myself, cumulatively waiting for all the promises to be enacted. What a different society this would be if even the war on poverty had been won, let alone all the other gobble-d-gook wars that have been promised, lost and forgotten. How can we ever expect to accomplish anything permanent if we stop and start projects so frivolously? We have become so jaded and mentally muscle-bound, however, we do not seem to realize that we are in mortal danger from our own refusal to form a serious government. The leadership we have now perpetrates narrow politicized decisions trumping everything else, even the expensive scientific or expert studies initiated by the government itself. This is analogous to making important decisions by reading entrails the way the Romans did. We think this had a lot to do with money not being spent properly to prevent the devastation exacted by Katrina. The brown shirts of G. W. Bush are, as fast as they judiciously can, dismantling a wide spectrum of intelligent government programs that disagree with their political view. It seems like everyday, they chip away at something new. Even though "what is intelligent" according to your political view is subjective, wiping out much of the equalitarian settled democratic gains the people have made in the years since the new deal without any regard as to whether it makes sense according to science or any other accepted standard is not intelligent. It's rule by prejudice. The problem is these Bush 2 radicals are not intelligent. They base their decisions on a prejudice against real democracy. They fear the competition of effective government. They intend to continue doing what they are doing until our system and everything we stand for is ruined. With this administration, the presidency has come close to being a dictatorship, because there seems to be no protection of any rights, let alone minority rights. Their main mission is to weaken government so that corporations can victimize the American people.

There are two terms for government that are used interchangeably to characterize government America style. The first type is called democracy and is defined as direct participation of all members of society in the legislative process. The second type of American government by definition is the republic form. Democracy in practice in America really means the republic form of government that allows the people a voice not directly, but through others who purport to represent their interests. In either case, what has become known, as American democracy is representative government that is supposed to represent people and their interests. This is characterized by the protection of individual and minority rights against any kind of dictatorship. The ultimate purpose of all democracy is to do the greatest good for the greatest number.

Another type of government is called despotism or dictatorship, or any other form of rule set up by a small clique or even majority, to do the greatest good for the least number, who are members of the ruling clique; like a business. Despotic government is turning government into a business to benefit the few. As we have proclaimed, with I think a fair degree of accuracy, some, if not many contemporary governments are businesses that are being run for the benefit of the few.

How does American democracy sync with these definitions of government? The individual American has been disenfranchised of representation because the majority of the congressional representatives no longer represent the rights of individuals in their district. The governing majority in congress does not represent people, but special interests, mainly corporate and other business and also including unions. Under the present form of American representative government, it is just a question of whether the government in power is going to allow maximum or minimum exploitation of people by special interests. The liberals and conservatives of both parties represent, respectively, liberal minimum exploitation or conservative maximum exploitation. This is because there is an oligarchic elite, if you will, who are really pulling the strings of government behind the scenes. They control the so-called representatives of the people, because they control the purse strings that put these people in office. These office holders are front men paid to fool the people into thinking they are on their side. The opposite is of course the rule. The American government then, according to the above definitions of democracy and dictatorship is representative dictatorship. That is what we have in America today. The great challenge for democracy today then is to reverse this by harnessing the corporate machine to man's needs instead of the other way around. Whatever it takes, the corporation must be de-fanged, domesticated, and made to do the master's bidding. That won't be easy. To accomplish this goal, representative dictatorship must be transformed into representative democracy by excising the corporation from the political process. If they've done it in Texas, we can do it in the whole country; Tom DeLay's successful corruption of the Texas system notwithstanding. The technical possibility of achieving this utopian ideal is now a reality sitting like a nubile virgin waiting to be deflowered but not despoiled. We the people must soon decide whether we are going to forever be dupes of the corporate controlled state or the masters. The only thing we have to fear is a beautiful nubile virgin robot. I predict

one of the great issues of the 21st century is going to be marriages

between humans and robots. Especially same sex robot marriage!

What hope or pipedream are we being sold under the label of the

present so-called conservative agenda? (At least this was true until the

06 midterms. Read this because they'll probably be back in two years.

Also, many new democrats are conservatives) Let us examine the

domestic program. It is claimed that things are booming, based mainly

on corporate profits and the Dow averages that have been climbing

until recently, 11/6/06. I don't agree. It is also claimed that

unemployment is low and in fact is too low and will cause inflation.

This fear is causing interest rates to be raised to cool this claimed

undesirably rapid growth. This upon close analyses seems to be

another distortion of the truth; unless you want to call low paying

service jobs and minimum pay jobs a full safe employment number.

This is what ninety percent of the new jobs are. I think on the contrary

there is a job depression that is being covered up by statistical

chicanery. The questions should be; are these new subsistence jobs

with low purchasing power likely to cause a permanent underclass and

can people be upgraded to better paying jobs Americans have

traditionally held? I think there is a big problem and the answer lies elsewhere.

The way the Republican Party apparently sees it is that we can just keep reducing taxes until the government pays us instead of us paying the government. Do not ask how much you owe the government; ask how much the government owes you. I hope I am not plagiarizing anybody, but you must admit, rhetoric works almost as well backwards as it does forwards. If inflation and bankruptcy ruin the economic system, having more money will not help much. You will need a truckload of money to pay for a newspaper. And contrary to the idea that heavy taxation is counterproductive, the Swedes feel quite the opposite and prefer to keep their extraordinarily high taxation in spite of their having the same economic problems as almost everybody else. In fact, the extremely high taxation rate did not seem to have any adverse effect at all in Sweden while there was prosperity. The Swedes believe that high taxation that is returned in services is very beneficial to their peace of mind and is not the cause of their economic malaise. They decided that the cause of their economic problem was becoming non-competitive in the world market. Keeping this problem at bay is a top priority.

I think we should try to find an optimum point of taxation in America and I think we should try to cut government waste and fat; however, the method by which this is carried out depends on the philosophy of government: i.e. what responsibility government must assume for the well-being of the public, better known as the general welfare. If it is believed that all services to the people are a waste of money except ones that are for people that belong to the party in power, then much less money is required to operate government. Of course this is not egalitarian democracy and, in fact, is dictatorship, even if the dictator has been elected by a majority of the people. If you think that reaching an optimum point of least taxation is more important than the government being able to have enough money to solve otherwise insolvable problems, then by all means let us have the least taxes. This is pre-Jefferson Federalism pure and simple. But, would not closing tax loopholes bring in more money to the government? Yes, but the point is, the government has more money than it can spend wisely, according to the pundits of conservative wisdom, and the rich people must have capital to finance the growth of the economy or our economy will degenerate, say these same wise men. Maybe the problem is that our taxes have never been high enough or our priorities worthy enough nor our sights moral enough to solve our problems. Clearly, higher taxes alone are not the solution, either. If we had the benefits for our taxes the Swedes have we would be still be faced with the same problem the Swedes have... and we already have, even though our social services are minimal; a faltering economy that cannot with economic sanity any longer finance the cradle-to-grave security we would like to have gotten used to forever. Clearly, then, unless we can find some answer for the problem of economic competition, our following the Swedish model of democracy, although probably the best in the world would be suicidal for us, since like health care, we cannot seem to finance our own minimal services to our people.

Can we then, create a viable energetic expansion to a full employment economy? I believe the answer is no, unless we are willing to make some drastic changes in our economy and in the world economy. There is one very basic and important economic law that the concept of putting more money into circulation ignores. The velocity of money. It is not the quantity of money; it's the motion that counts. It is not how much money is available that is most important; it is how fast the money circulates that is crucial. The housing industry goes dead if people cannot borrow money because of high interest rates. If everyone who wanted a house in this country could suddenly afford to finance the building of a house, there would instantly be millions of new jobs. If the money made available by a tax cut lays in bank accounts, is exported overseas where it can be employed more profitably or is used for any purpose except business expansion and job creation in America, it will not result in an energetically expanding American economy that can save us from lingering chronic underemployment. In the Great Depression, there was total financial stagnation. Money did not circulate because financial institutions feared to lend money in an economy that provided for no certainty about anything. It is true that business must have money to expand. So do individuals or governments. But there are other relevant issues to economic expansion. I do not think an influx of capital is going to result in a rapid expansion of American business because its competition abroad is too strong and growing stronger by the day. The only way American business is going to have the possibility of real high quality job expansion is if it is given high tariff protection or if the dollar drops so much in value that American goods will be so cheap they will be able to compete favorably with foreign goods. Right now, the worm has turned and the dollar has been dropping, which looks good for our balance of payments, but there is no guarantee of how far it will drop or when it will go back up. The ups and downs of the dollar is an unpredictable element at best. Of course, increased tariffs would be a disaster for the global free trade economy, for American prestige and for multi-national domination of world trade.

It would seem that the simplest and, therefore, in all probability most simplistic solution would be to hope for a degradation of the dollar. Political expediency, however, dictates that we protect the dollar. If the dollar drops drastically, the Arabs, the Asians and others might not accept dollars for their exports to America, thus upsetting the international monetary system based on the dollar. Tariff barriers to free trade are unthinkable because they would result in a worldwide tariff war, which could have a crippling effect on an already precariously tenuous world trade dependent on exports. It is also supposed to be a basic economic fact that every country benefits by producing what can be most efficiently produced in that country and selling to countries that cannot as efficiently produce that product. So every country benefits to some degree by importing products from abroad. This is known as the law of comparative advantage. However, it is a fallacious law in my view. The problem is that this does not balance out the way it is supposed to. Many countries have no advantage in anything. Manufacturing industry produces a lot more wealth per man-hour than does production of agriculture or raw materials, other than oil and some minerals. Oil, which has recently become a scarce resource as well as a necessity of life, has become so expensive that it has made a few countries rich in this resource fabulously wealthy while it threatens to disrupt and destroy the economy of the rest of the world. If some cheap replacement is not soon found, I think everyone is aware that the present world economy is doomed. Free trade based on comparative advantage is an economic hoax unless you count having workers you can exploit enough to under price other countries comparative advantage. This is the tipping scale factor in current world economic competition. There is now neither fair competition nor balance, because the world economy is based on economic rape of one country by another. This is an intolerable situation and cannot go on much longer without total calamity to what is known as world free trade. You can already see the reaction coming from Latin America where several countries have recently installed left wing governments hostel to U.S. policies. America cannot improve its economic position, therefore, by imposing tariffs on its friends and trading partners and risk world economic chaos; and it cannot deflate the dollar without causing other drastic economic-political crises to exporting countries. Therefore, it is my contention that the American economy is a muscle-bound disaster lacking crucial flexibility to make adjustments to its economy because of political considerations.

Bush's economic policies then, because their main concern is to make it possible for business to expand, are asinine and simplistic, because the American economy, due to present limitations put on it by considerations of political expediency, is unnaturally limited. And the same limitations exist whether you are a liberal or a conservative. The failure of politicians is a failure to realize we have created a muscle-bound economy that cannot compete effectively enough to keep us from withering away industrially. The energy companies are a good test case. With a huge new supply of capital, most of them do not need outside government capital for oil exploration so they are using the money to pay for golden parachutes and buy already existing companies that will in no way solve the energy problem or increase employment. It just increases monopoly. At the same time they are some of the greatest beneficiaries of the recent tax cuts in spite of the fact they clearly have more than enough capital to run their own stores and then some. This kind of lunatic policymaking, including relying on these companies to supply R & D for alternative energy sources that will be competitors, smacks of loony idiocy for my money. Even for Bush 2, this give away is beyond the pale of any rational explanation in my view.

It is clear that if we are going to continue our policy of providing a military umbrella for the whole friendly part of the world at the same time that we are sacrificing our economy for political expediency, we are headed toward economic disaster. It is obvious to all, but our political leaders, that if we do not soon put our house in order there isn't going to be any house to put in order. Perhaps this last statement is a little irrationally rash, but chagrin with what to me are nutty policies has the effect of leading to nutty conclusions. I apologize if this is over the top. I think everyone is somewhat aware, including our leaders, that there are problems, especially with becoming more competitive. The difference is, and I think it is a crucial difference, is that I do not think there is a correct understanding of what the problem is or what corrective action should be taken. And if we do not find out soon, it is going to be economic Armageddon right here on earth and our worst fears may come true.

Are tariffs and devaluing the dollar in any way viable solutions to the problem of creating fair competition and a balanced world economy? We believe such drastic steps would create so much havoc for our allies and client states that such a step is really unthinkable. This would not only have terrible political consequences for us, but would certainly be as economically counterproductive as such measures have been in the past. There would no doubt be a contraction of the world economy that might, in fact, spell the end of the world free enterprise system. The end of it in its present form, however, is an inevitability.

Then what are we to do? We seem to have only two alternatives. To watch our economy go down the drain, as we have been doing, or risk abandoning a free trade world market economy we consider a graven in stone necessity. I think there has to be an alternative to these poor choices, and I do have a third solution to offer that I think is a radical (Radical is not always a bad word) departure from these other two choices. If utilized, it will require an entirely new world economic order. The idea is based on the moral concept of fair play. What I recommend is that we require the price of all imports that are deemed in competition with domestically produced products of the same quality to be on a competitive par in price with American products of the same class. If other countries do the same, this will create fair and equal worldwide competition between countries that are now competing on a hilly playing field unfairly for the same world market. The effect of this economic ploy would hopefully be to have the protectionist benefits of a tariff, without the punitive effect of a tariff for revenue. I call this idea Parity Economics. Why such a drastic step to create fair competition? The main problem with the American economy is that our domestic companies cannot compete on a level playing field fair basis with products made in a country that has few social benefits such as health care, pensions and other things included in worker pay, and allows its workers to be paid much lower wages, subsidizes its industry or does other things to ensure that it has a favorable competitive position in relation to the industries of other countries. The problem of the American economy is the same as the problem of the Swedish economy, except the greater Swedish social development magnifies the Swedish problem and creates a worse problem for the Swedes than probably anyone else. The paradox of the current world economic order is that the more democracy you have, the less economically competitive is your economy. Obviously, unless this situation is corrected, it will encourage more and more world despotism and less and less of the democratic reforms that are becoming prohibitively expensive. Under the present unfair global free market system we cannot compete at home or abroad effectively enough to have a prosperous, expanding economy that will pay for a democratic social order offering security and other social benefits. We are withering on the vine of coolie competition... unfair and unwise, and so is most of the rest of the world. All to line the pockets of transnational corporations.

Think of a reverse tariff to understand economic parity. If Volvo wants to sell cars in America, it must charge the same price for a Volvo as is charged for a comparable American car. If an American automaker wants to compete with Volvo, it must charge the same thing for a car in the same class in Sweden as Sweden charges. What I am not talking about is not requiring America, Sweden or Japan to charge the same thing for a motor scooter or mini-car as is charged for a full size car in a totally different class. This would just be another form of unfair competition. I am also not talking about charging the same thing for bananas grown in a country that must grow them in a hothouse as is charged by a country where they grow naturally. This would be foolish, unfair protection. I am quite simply talking about requiring equal competition between industrial nations in products that should cost nearly the same to produce if all workers were paid the same fair wage and everyone bought resources to manufacture these goods for about the same price. The more efficient producer will receive a small windfall that it deserves. The less efficient producer will justifiably price himself out of the market.

Is this not the same as charging a tariff? It most certainly is not, for many reasons. Tariffs traditionally are intended to make all competition unfair. Requiring a Parity of price is not only a way of creating fair competition, it is a way of reducing monopoly and creating new fair competition. Not for any reason is it fair to require companies that have higher costs they cannot control (Often necessary democratic costs) to compete at a higher price for their products that people are unwilling to pay. Obviously, the comparable quality higher priced product will lose out just on the basis of price. We are now paying the highest price of all for such foolish non-competitive competition: loss of high quality employment, elimination of pensions and other benefits and drastic contraction of our industrial base. And this kind of stupid non-competitive competition we have accepted as the norm, fortifies one of the worst moral problems of capitalism as articulated by Karl Marx. It encourages employers and governments to keep the wages and benefits of their workers as artificially low as possible to be in a favorable competitive position. The Japanese, the Taiwanese, the Hong Kong Chinese, our good friends the Koreans and, now, our new "partners" the mainland Chinese, often in partnership with foreign capitalists, have been, taking advantage of their lesser social development to exploit their workers and pay lower wages than the socially developed nations of Europe and North America can. Not that we are angels who have not done the same thing in the past and may well again in the future if it becomes possible for the corporate dictatorship to degrade Americans any further before we wake up and punish the culprits. However, I think we now know the real reason democratic rights and reforms are being cut to a minimum in America. Our people and workers are paying a heavy price for allowing our companies to uncontrollably export capital and technology overseas. Our people must become more like coolies in order that our industry can regain the position of being number one predator of the world. We have additionally reduced the quality of our products to compete and that hasn't worked either. It has only given a bad name to our product's quality. This is what really is wrong with Ford and GM. Now we must reduce the quality of our lives to compete. And finally, unless we change to a parity economy that will allow for industrial expansion of our manufacturing base, we must auto genocide ourselves out of existence by taking more and better birth control pills, because a third world import economy will not support the quality jobs our family lifestyle has become accustomed to. Something is happening out there Mr. Jones, and now you know what it is. You are not needed anymore. And just in time for the Catholic Church to start handing out rubbers.

Of course, under a system of Parity, the Asians and others who live in substandard housing and eat a predominantly cheap vegetarian diet, will not be able to run away with the world economy, as they are now doing because we are not competing with them, but are capitulating to them. Ironically, they are low-balling us in the world economy by obstructing the import of our goods while we, the people of America, are subsidizing their economies by paying much of their military bill.

(Except for mainland China) I do not want to leave the impression I am putting down Japanese or other Asians for their lifestyle that I think compares most favorably with the Western lifestyle. It is healthier to eat a predominantly vegetarian diet and it is healthier to live close to the hard floor. Unfortunately, most Americans still prefer not too change their high fat killer diets and comfy beds for a smarter more Spartan lifestyle. After all, we have Lipitor, treadmills and bloody surgeons to save us. It is also a lot cheaper. This, however, is a small factor in why we are unable to compete with Asian industry. Japan used to be 50 years ago, if it is not still, the cleanest, most charming country in the world. They are fine people and certainly deserve all of their success. However, we Americans must wake up and think about our own economic survival.

Another reason parity will not have the same effect, as a tariff is that it will not be an onerous collection of money from foreign products at all. And because Nike and others will collect more money for the same products, it will bring pressure for Nike to pay its employees on a par with American workers and generally have the desirable effect of putting workers all over the world on a par with one another. At least there will not be an incentive any longer to exploit workers just so products can be sold cheaper in America. Also, unlike a tariff, it will not be an excuse to protect an inferior local product. It will quite simply have the effect of giving everyone a chance to compete on a level playing field basis and be an incentive to create quality products. Pollution and safety devices can be installed on cars without manufacturers having to fear that the increased price will make a company's product less competitive. It would have, in some cases, an anti-inflationary effect, because economies of mass production (The more you make, the less it costs to produce) would allow the possibilities of lower prices. Conversely, the less we are producing today, the more that has to be charged for a product. It would enable new businesses to start that could immediately compete with foreign imports. For example, an American T.V. manufacturer could begin production of a television set at a price that would immediately give the American company a guaranteed fair profit

that in all probability would cause the other TV importers to raise their prices slightly to put them on a par. Other things being equal, this would ensure the survival and competitiveness of the American product. Also, this would encourage foreign importers to open plants in the U.S. to compete, as some are already doing.

At first the American consumer will be unhappy to pay a slightly higher price but, at least in the long run, he might have a job and income that he could not have had if the present situation continues. The American consumer is just deluding himself that it is cheaper to buy imported consumer products we could be making ourselves; because if there were a lot more jobs his salary and real income would be much higher. But people being people, me included, we will continue to rip-off our fellow workers and ourselves until the system is changed and it costs the same for an American product as it does for foreign imports. By this method, we can preserve the competitiveness of our economy and not punish the whole world for the shortsightedness of our leaders. It will also take the pressure off of companies that are jumping on the present trend of capitalism to cannibalize its worker's benefits in order to achieve a competitive edge or just survive. America, at present should declare bankruptcy, because of a trade deficit and budget deficit combined approaching two trillion a year. See Professor Laurence Kotlikoff's research for the Federal Reserve Bank of St. Louis. According to his central analysis, "the US is already bankrupt, insofar as it will be unable to pay its creditors...". Parity Economics will allow America to reverse this trend. Every country in the world will truly have an opportunity to establish a real economy. Instead of empty words about comparative advantage, each country can best produce whatever it wishes without the fear of being overwhelmed and bankrupted by the unfair competition of giant transnational capitalist-socialist predatory corporate empires. The way they are presently operating, they are the real evil empires, overwhelming national governments with the power of their money. The only way this can be permanently reformed is to make it unprofitable to bribe politicians. Fair Parity pricing of products is a good way to make a start.

If we do not get our house in order and breathe new life into our disintegrating economy, we are never going to be able to tackle the immense problems at home and abroad that are either threatening our existence or that, like space exploration and basic research, will dramatically improve our existence if we spend the money to make it happen. Man can do anything if the resources are available to him. When we discover a cheap new source of energy, and we will if we make it a priority, there will be no limit to man's possibilities; but we are way overdue for that breakthrough. We cannot wait and fight like dogs over a bone for the last drop of oil. The situation has already disrupted the world economy to an inordinate degree. Unless we find a cheap practical source of energy the good life we now know in a small part of the world will be out of reach, forever, for the billions in this world that yearn for it. This cannot be and will not be. Humanity will break its chains and the backs of its oppressors no matter who they are.

Not only can we solve our problems if we properly apply ourselves; we can create a utopia of material security, abolish illness as a reason for death and possibly even abolish death itself. There is no limitation on what science can accomplish. The limitations are those humanity, and especially humanity's leaders, place on man. Man only reaps what he sows. We are now planting 99% of the seeds of our own destruction. What a different world this would be if that misdirected 99% of our energy could be put to building a people world. The American people are generous, but many have been driven to dropping out of the political process entirely by a political leadership that has betrayed the democratic ideal, an ideal that has always given this country the thrusting power to move forward and stay on top. We have been betrayed into the hands of a corporate despotism that has made life too expensive for the average little man to enjoy. The forgotten man of Roosevelt is the lost person of Bush. The American little man has never been willing to be made a coolie for long. We Americans, and for that matter, all the people of the world, deserve something better than "have" and "have not" nations based on unfair competition. We in America cannot idly sit back and watch our entire economy erode away to foreign competition. We also cannot expect other nations to sit idly by and have us preempt the entire world economy. There must be a new balance struck someway or "a hard rains agonna fall", whether it is acid or nuclear fallout.

It is my belief that America always has to be the best. Not so we can be big-headed, ugly Americans who take credit for more than we deserve, but so we can take genuine pride in representing the best values that exist on the face of the earth. Two hundred years ago we represented the best. Today in the important arena of political-economic development we are retarded in many ways. We have a pseudo democracy that is inhibiting progress at home and abroad. We have a media that is a handmaiden to the political elite, because it is not independent. The sciences are not truly respected or their findings utilized. Even the movies seldom reach the culturally embellishing level of art that they have the capacity for, because profit is more of a concern of the companies providing funding to make them than is art. Real art is extremely important, because it communicates truth. Truth cures society of some of its pervasive insanity. This is very important. Pseudo art communicates illusion, which is not important, except as escape or entertainment. Although, it is my belief that America must blaze the way to the future by spending the money necessary to solve the crucial problems of energy, poverty, health, population explosion in the third world, space, environment and other important problems requiring expensive attention, I would also like to see America become the "brains of the world" and not the "bully of the world.

Sticking our heads in the ground like ostriches cannot solve our problems. In the age of super multi-national corporations, we must have a super socialist capitalist powerhouse economy that will ensure every American a decent standard of living and cradle-to-grave security. We must have a strong, efficient, loving government committed to individual freedom, a government rich enough and big enough to solve all problems that cannot be delegated to private enterprise without penalizing the people. And I am afraid many of these problems have reached critical mass. There is no time to waste. The plan for this government is the subject of the last two chapters of this book.

Chapter 7

Parity Manifesto

The Parity Party Manifesto is an attempt to form a democratic political consensus for a people-oriented party that is a clear alternative to the oligarchic corporation oriented parties that only pretend to represent the people and, in fact, mainly represent moneyed special interests. All backing from such interests, along with any representatives of such interest, will be prohibited from this party. We are to be true partisans of the people. At the same time, we reject dictatorship of any kind, be it proletarian pseudo socialism or capitalist pseudo democracy. Our main objective is to bring about an individualist democracy that will ensure every forgotten little person cradle-to-grave security, and make possible his or her fulfillment in life by constitutional guarantees of jobs, health, education, personal choice and personal freedom. It is a political-social-economic ideology that will attempt to end the bloodthirsty dichotomy between socialism and capitalism by presenting a pragmatic alternative that will be a synthesis of both. Its slogan will be: Parity People Power Now!

The ideological war between capitalism and socialism has seemed to become a thing of the past at the present time, momentarily eclipsed by the war on terror. This is only temporary however. As long as there are polarized rich and poor, these ideologies are always going to be in contention. For a while the cold war was so destructive that most of the fruits of humanity's labor were being squandered on arms buildup and surrogate wars that threatened the future of life on this planet. With the collapse of the communist Soviet Union and its replacement based on capitalist democracy, however, the peace between these two ideologies that has resulted seems more like a truce than peace. It would not be surprising if there were an unfortunate reversion to cold war ideologies. The surviving adherents of both systems still protest a belief that its ideology is superior to the other. We believe this is not true and that each ideology working together has certain benefits that can be brought to bear, which can indispensably improve the lot of humanity. It is my belief that Parityism can incorporate the best elements of socialism and capitalism and create a hybrid super-capitalist-socialism that is better than either alone. This can be the nexus for genuine democracy. I resolutely believe that this super-capitalist-socialism dedicated to the proposition that everyone has a right to the opportunity for the fulfillment of his life holds forth the possibility of becoming the first real democracy in the history of the world. It is believed super-capitalist-socialism can cure the confused morality of contemporary civilization by replacing the false worship of greed with a worship of the one undeniable god, nature. The laws of nature should be the basis of all political, economic and social law. The rights of man and his environment should be protected by adherence to these natural laws, as known to science. The main purpose of government should be to give man access to the means to equality based on the right to fulfill his or her life. In the interest of incentive and creativity, most of man's economic activity should be free of government interference. Government should be required to guarantee a Parity economic pricing of goods and services based on fair competition. Fair competition should be defined as based on a level playing field of competition between nations.

It is believed that such a new political-social-economic philosophy is necessary to protect and expand the rights of the individual, because individual rights have been preempted by both private and collective enterprise. A new definition of democratic rights is also needed, because the concept of democracy is murky, ambiguous and poorly understood by the masses of humanity, and in its present manifestation is really only an illusion of democracy created to give man a false sense of security and freedom. This is true whether the ownership of the means of production is wielded privately or collectively. In the case of collective ownership, which is supposed to be ownership by the people, the ownership by the people is pseudo fake ownership, because the real ownership is in the hands of a small clique of tyrants who use the fruits of that ownership to aggrandize themselves and the state at the expense and impoverishment of the people. We call all systems that now represent the human race and claim to be democratic or socialist, pseudo democracy or pseudo socialism. What we must have, if we are ever to bring general humanity to a level of happiness based on justice, is a democracy that respects, encourages and makes competitively possible individual industry.

It is believed that the confusion in America over the real meaning of democracy has allowed the evolvement of an inefficient, ineffectual government suffering from sclerotic laws and controlled by self-interest groups, especially the corporations that do not have the best interests of the people in mind. It is believed that the Democratic Party that purports to represent the huddled masses in America, has demonstrated an unwillingness to make a total commitment to solve the problems of quality employment, costly housing in cities, the danger of the military-industrial-government complex and an energy policy that has America a hostage to unreliable countries. These and other problems have been ignored while the liberals have attempted to eradicate poverty by putting in place a modified dole system to support the victims of this system who cannot find jobs that will support them and their families. This too has not proved to be successful in liberating the poor from poverty. A so-called conservative approach to solving America's vast problem of dependency on the government dole adopted by both mainstream political parties has attempted to replace the automatic entitlement of financial support with an earned entitlement that has required the recipients of the dole to train for a job. This approach has had some degree of success, but the jobs are mostly low-end minimum wage jobs that do not usually save the person from a life of poverty.

The Republican conservative's entire philosophy of government is an exercise in negative thinking. They believe the best government is the least government. Even though staunchly anti-Marxist, their approach to government is, paradoxically analogous to utopian Marxism that claims that if the state withers away or according to GOP hype is downsized to almost nothing, everybody will be much better off. Since coming to power under George W. Bush, the neo-conservatives, like the Democrats before them, not only haven't reduced the size of government, they have increased it a great deal, proving once again the innate hypocrisy and downright lies and stupidity of campaign promises. In both cases of anarchistic GOP conservatism and Marxism, we are convinced this is wishful, simplistic and suicidal thinking propagated for the hypocritical purpose of gaining power. The present administration is proceeding to daily whittle away in every way at the foundations of democracy. The result will not be power to the people, but more power to the faction already most powerful, the rich. In all forms of government that exist in the world today, there is one cardinal rule. If the people's rights are not adequately protected, the result is tyranny. As far as I can see, nowhere are the people's rights adequately protected.

I think the American poor people should wake up and realize they deserve something better than the choice of the vicious circle welfare dole that doesn't offer much hope of a better life for its recipients or the alternative of a stingy earned entitlement to bottom of the barrel jobs. This is a small improvement on the do-nothing past of conservative thinking, but none of this is going to create a vibrant strong America.

The promise of tax cuts is a false promise. The claims made of economic turn-a-rounds caused by tax cuts are a false claim. It is the normal business cycle, not the tax cuts that are curing or causing recessions. (Not that I am totally rejecting Keynesian methods. It has its place) This pump priming cannot be more than a stopgap measure anyway unless we concurrently solve the problems of underemployment and economic malaise. After we spend the money and the government has no money, there will not be prosperity, but depression. America is on the road to third world status. The port of Long Beach/L.A., Ca., the busiest American port, largely services imports of finished consumer goods and machinery from Asia and mainly exports recyclable garbage and raw materials, according to a harbormaster interviewed on local T.V. She is also quoted as saying this is a formula of a third world country, as indeed it is. And we are the busiest port in the nation.

America, from being by far the richest country in the world, is gradually sliding into economic and political chaos because of misguided politically expedient policies that have allowed our economy to be exported or displaced by foreign competitors. Our leaders have failed to anticipate overwhelming problems like the energy crunch, and are attempting to provide a police force for the whole free world. About all this is accomplishing is to subsidize our economic competitors. A Japanese official, in an unusually candid statement for the usually very diplomatic Japanese, stated that the American thirst for military spending is unquenchable. How well we American taxpayers know. I just cannot wait for another billion dollar plane to roll off the production line. Looks like we need a few more carriers to support wars on a few more continents instead of just enough (Ten) for two ocean conflicts. And we need to double or triple our military since our regular army seems to be tied up permanently as sitting ducks in Iraq and Korea. (I was part of it in Korea 50 years ago and we're still there) I hear the penguins in Antarctica are marching around getting pretty uppity. Maybe we should send an aircraft carrier and straighten them out. God help us! America the beautiful is now

America the muddled. If only we could get those planes to run on penguin pee.

We have failed to anticipate and deal effectively with our major problems because government in America, whether liberal or conservative, has an inferiority complex. It is the belief of American lawmakers, especially the conservatives that government is at best an ineffectual substitute for anything that private enterprise can do; and it is believed that private enterprise can do anything better than government. This is a false and misguided ideology best illustrated by the energy problem. Because of government reliance on the efficacy of private enterprise, no one bothered to anticipate the multiplicity of different energy problems now occurring. It was not and is still not in the best interest of the private oil industry to sound the alarm about the energy shortage problem. Solar energy or some other form of cheap energy is competition to those entrenched oil companies that certainly would not benefit if we could say cheaply make combustible fuel from the hydrogen in sea water. Consequently, no one, because of this failure to assume responsibility by government for unanticipated emergencies bothered to anticipate something as obvious as retaliation against us for policies of ours detested by Muslim governments. Until we have a government that understands that it has to anticipate and solve major problems before they get out of control, our country is going to continue to crumble. If in our weakened state, we no longer have the financial assets necessary to cope, there is a high probability that our problems are never going to be solvable. Business can no longer solve all the problems of a complex civilization such as ours without the cooperation of government and people. It cannot do the job alone, if it ever could. Business cannot rebuild cities that people do not have the money to pay for. Business may not always be able to provide jobs that are being lost to automation or competition or business contraction or any other reason fast enough to prevent catastrophe. The concept of a safety net for providing a bottom line of security for the poor is pure nonsense of the talk is cheap variety Bush is so fond of. By the standards real democracy is supposed to stand for, the present shrinking safety net is an inadequate joke. Our safety net is just a euphemism for soaking the poor to protect the rich.

Business must begin to change its rapacious nature and view itself as a partner in the process of building a strong healthy country, both morally and economically. It must keep itself honest, patriotic and entirely separate from the coercion and corruption of government over which it now, unduly and unhealthily for the best interests of the people, exercises a decisive influence. At the same time, business must be helped to be more viable for appropriate economic expansion, by the passing of government legislation that mandates fair competition between American companies and foreign companies selling products on our soil. The object of economic expansion should be the job formation of not just the quantity of jobs, but also the quality of jobs. After such laws creating a parity of competition are in place, government should provide funds, through a reindustrialization finance agency, for the appropriate job creating expansion of the American manufacturing business that is practically extinct.

The process of creating a Parity pricing system will at the same time have the positive protectionist effect of a tariff to protect beginning industries without the adverse effect of destroying world free trade or constraining consumer choice. (Of course, it will temporarily make prices higher on some items) This plan will provide a climate in which fair worldwide competition can take place among all nations for a share of the world market, even the smallest nation. It should have the very desirable effect of reducing the gap economically between "have" and "have not" nations, because it will be in the self-interest of every nation to develop its own local industry in which workers will be paid according to what should become a standard international wage. It is now in the self-interest of nations to underpay their workers to have a favorable competitive position in the world market. It is believed that by the promulgation of such simple policies, the present trend toward the disintegration and displacement of American business can be reversed, and the groundwork laid for a supercapitalistsocialism that will provide enough wealth for a real bottom line of guaranteed employment of every human being in this country and elsewhere.

Stopping at this point, however, would not be a Parityism fair deal. It would just be a new kind of more evolved liberal conservatism (Maybe real conservatism) that would more intelligently employ the resources of a stronger government than is usually associated with conservatism in this country. I think the present people who erroneously call themselves conservatives are preponderantly radical pirates in pinstriped suits. They are in other words, freebooters who care nothing for the well being of their fellow man, the epitome of the selfish agents of greed. We must make possible a super-capitalist-socialist economic powerhouse that can fund a true democratic equality for all its citizens such as that which follows.

Chapter 8.

The New Parity Synthesis

The democratic individualist equality of Parityism is based on a triad of self-development guarantees, which include guaranteed full employment, guaranteed major health care, and a guaranteed free college level education that will qualify a person for a fulfilling job. This means that each person must have a chance to reach his or her full potential.

Obviously, everyone who wants to be a movie star or an astronaut cannot be one, even under the full potential development concept of Parityism. There have to be certain practical limitations on any idea of freedom because the opportunists and predators will given the chance have a field day and turn any pearl into a sows ear. These limitations should be based on what is pragmatically possible. The bottom line, however, should be an extension of free education to include higher education, including graduate school, for those who qualify by testing for the best talent. Testing to qualify for higher education must become part of the American system. Trying to educate everyone equally is just another form of stupid pseudo democratic posturing to impress on Americans that they have real democracy when they don't.

Trying to educate everyone ends up educating no one. It is a self-fulfilling prophecy to say Americans don't make good scientists when they are not encouraged properly. The incentive to excel is quashed when there is a culture of leveling mediocrity that doesn't sort out talent. There is also a great deal of uncertainty about qualifying for and financing such an education. Financing such an education by borrowing from Fanny Mae is almost a certainty to cause you to end up with bad credit, according to a 60 minutes expose I saw recently. If your credit is bad, no one on A list will hire you even if you have the best education in the world. Our government unashamedly doesn't blink at this over the top obscene exploitation of our students by usurious loan sharks. It's the ultimate form of privatization when you get to make money without any risk at the same time any deadbeat student borrowers can be ruined with usurious interest rates. Fanny Mae customers have no recourse for release from debt, as the loans are exempt from bankruptcy laws. Wow, how more putridly self-damning can our system become? What's behind this negative propaganda about American's aptitudes for science is that it's much cheaper all the way around to use H-1B and import talent. These are two egregious examples of corporations being allowed to fatten their bottom line at the expense of security and quality of life in America.

For those who do not qualify or want a higher education, some sort of apprenticeship program based on trade school training must be made available to those who want it. An apprenticeship program has been very effective in West Germany in reducing unemployment among the young and supplying skilled workers to German industry. Coordinating such training with the newly established Parity industries financed by government or private enterprise would be one good way to attack the unemployment problem. There is nothing that has ever paid more dividends to a society than education. Today, more than any other time in history, everyman must have some kind of extensive formal or trade education in order to fit into our complicated, modern world. Most of those chronically unemployed are also unskilled and undereducated. Everyone must have some skill, whether it is manual or intellectual, in order to find a niche in today's pecking order. And there is nothing that creates equality faster than education. How many stories have we heard about the high achiever immigrant who came to America to get a free education? (Elia Kazan's "America America", an autobiographical film, is a most stunning example) As we were saying, many come here, or used to, to get a free education. Our system of education in the past, probably illustrated what American democracy stood for better than anything else. That same schooling today is a meaningless symbol compared to what it used to be, because the free part of that schooling today is about on a par with what no schooling was in the past. What good is it to be able to read the newspaper if you cannot get a job. That is why America today is a lot less equal than it used to be and, therefore, a lot less democratic. It is one of the glaring discrepancies in the democratic process that an American free education has become meaningless. Higher education, which should certainly be free to the qualified, is by no means the complete answer itself. And it is becoming prohibitively expensive to all but the rich.

The Germans, as mentioned, have an apprenticeship program that trains its youths for a trade or skill that will qualify them for a decent job in industry. In the case of either trade or higher education there must be equality of opportunity for those who qualify, or education will only be a cosmetic exercise in despotism. And of course there must be a match between training and jobs.

Those who qualify for higher education by competitive exam should not only receive a free education, but a stipend to live on besides. This is how it should be. We should pay our gifted young to learn, because they will pay us back later with more productive lives. In lieu of this ideal being possible, financing should be made to those who qualify that will not be an insurmountable burden. We don't want our young to have to begin life with bad credit or in bankruptcy court. We are doing the opposite now. Bush 2. is tightening the screws on the amount of money available for college loans in his current budget proposals. God willing, he will see the light and change this. Unfortunately, he lacks the education or intelligence to either see the light or make wise choices. You cannot be totally ignorant of history, as he seems to be in spite of being a history major, and make good world-class decisions. As a not isolated example, he doesn't seem to know that democracies have not only started wars, but also started the worst one in history. Hitler was democratically elected. Bush's "administration" seems to have a propensity to make bad choices. Is this the hallmark of a C student? Maybe he wants to cut the education budget because he has a grudge against education. If the job he is doing is any indication, his didn't do much for him. Whatever the reason, it should be crystal clear that he is not smart enough to be president. That is not his fault, however. It is ours for electing him: or allowing the election to be stolen for him by the Supreme Court.

Sadly, you constantly meet people who have had their life's hopes dashed because they were unable to afford the education they desired and needed. This is an obscenely unfair situation that is all the more disgusting when you find out that some of the wealthy people going to college are going just for the status, fun, or some other frivolous reason. This is certainly an area of gross undemocratic inequality in America and gets worse every year. The rich can afford to warehouse their kids for whatever the reason at whatever the cost, but this is certainly not true for the middle class "near-do-wells". They are seriously stretched financially when they are faced with paying for offspring to go to expensive colleges, sometimes more than one at the same time.

The Parity equality manifesto stands for universal free education at all levels for those who qualify. We make our highest priority universal free education because, without a good education today, the hope of having a full life of employment is very slim and getting slimmer by the year, thanks mainly to rapid technological change that is happening at warp speed. Technological advance must be accepted as a part of the reality of the evolvement of man. What must not be accepted is that desirable technical evolvement must make most men obsolete and a few men masters of all. Of course, we can have plenty of employment in this country for some time to come if the unfair competition of pseudo free trade that is an impediment for our economy is changed. Maybe the rationale of members of congress for ignoring this injustice is that since they do not have to work no one else has to. The trouble is they get paid for doing nothing and very handsomely, indeed. (I have heard more than one say they are not given enough time to read most laws they vote on. If they don't do this, what do they do?) The whiny mantra of American politicians I love to hate is, "Except for the great sacrifice I am making serving the people, I could be making a lot more money in private industry". Yes, maybe, if you patiently spent years climbing the corporate ladder like other people. Or maybe some of them don't have the right stuff. Is that why many of them become lobbyists when they leave congress? The only thing, apparently, many of them can really do well after leaving government is corrupt the system by giving bribes to congress people in the form of campaign contributions. For this skullduggery, they are paid very well indeed. This "we don't get equal pay with private enterprise mantra" has been used as an excuse, especially at the state and local level to pay obscenely outrageous salaries and retirement to officials. The fleecing of the taxpayers in California is truly mind-boggling. The Sheriff of L.A. county gets almost as much as the President of the U.S. Over $350,000. He offered, to his credit, to give up his retirement pay portion from another public sector job, but was rebuffed. This kind of pay in California is not the exception, but the rule. There has to be some kind of Guinness record for the number of bureaucrats getting 100-150,000 paychecks, many for jobs that would be a joke in private industry. And their retirement pay, which usually almost equals or exceeds regular pay in Ca, is based on similar lame excuses that are an even worse obscenity. As Helen Thomas is wont to say, "Where are the outraged taxpayers?" I don't know. Maybe getting some rays. The truth is people have no say. The politicians of both parties are stonewalling the people with impunity and are getting away with it. Politicians are ruling by arrogance because they can. If you put one party out of office, the other turns out to be a worse nightmare. Why? Because the system is broken and people have become apathetic to political arrogance.

The most frank politician in recent memory I can think of was Jerry Ford who practically came out and said, he thought the Presidency of the United States was a kind of sinecure that required little or no work on his part. Consequently, he vetoed practically everything congress enacted that came his way, some 68 bills. Even though much of this had to do with inflation fighting, it is interesting because it implies he knew, from his experience being a leader in congress that most legislation being passed was mostly just sectional interest fluff, passed more to fool people into thinking they were getting bang for their bucks for electing people to congress. Also, just like the current (06) controversial immigration bills before congress that are being driven by popular demand, by the time the compromisers are finished with them, they will be truncated to meaningless hash. In this case, neither party wants to face the wrath of the minority that demographic statistics predict in about 40 years will be a majority in the U. S., by offending it. The Republicans paid the price in the recent midterm election losing about ten percent of their Latino demographic. (Also, the Latinos are already flexing their muscle with giant demonstrations opposing this legislation) The whole debate is an exercise in public relations to justify worming out of a political catch 22 that both parties do not want to deal with.

Another high-minded politician was a make work bureaucrat like Carter who read all the fine print except whether presidents get P.X. privileges. That is what I call unselfish devotion to duty. Carter, while morally high minded and hard working, may have allowed himself to be crushed under the weight of taking the job too seriously. It seems a president that does nothing and one that does too much come out about the same. Why? Because the institution is obsolete.

Parity, although recognizing the reality that most work known today may become obsolete in the next not so many years, stands very firmly for a full employment goal. People will always need jobs, because life is hell without work. We must therefore replace present jobs with other jobs just as relevant. We in America are going through a period of job anxiety. Maybe even job depression. There is no job security because of a worldwide distribution of technology and education that allows the same jobs to be performed in many different places, including third world countries. The jobs that are available are jobs that may not support a high standard of living that Americans are used to or feel they are entitled to. The solution to this problem may soon be the greatest issue politicians have to deal with if they want to be elected to office. We believe the only long-term solution to this problem is Parity Economics. There must be a guarantee of enough viable companies existing to provide enough jobs to employ the population. Only by using government muscle to guarantee the survival of employment entities can you guarantee full employment. The future is here. The problems today of outsourcing, shifting ownership of the means of production, quality of jobs and other economic job problems are just going to get worse until a fix is put in.

Once a Parity fix or other fix is put in that guarantees a viable economy, we need to consider the fine-tuning that will prevent the repugnant homogenization of people. People, who have a valuable and viable alternative to a regular job and have no desire for a regular 9-to-5er, should be granted a decent stipend income until their art, craft or other useful and valuable employment can be brought to fruition. No one should be required to be employed at work that is repugnant to them. And, of course, people who have skills, or for some reason are unable to attain skills, and cannot find work must be given a decent interim income, free from the hassle and stigma attached to welfare. People who do not want to help us build a better world, and there are really not as many as you might think, will be helped to become professional consumers. The more they consume, the more the rest of us can have fun making things. Of course, we must learn how to consume so we do not cannibalize our solar system. Even bad jokes should be upgraded and re-cycled. We cannot call ourselves a democracy until people who want to work are given employment of the kind they deserve to be doing.

Most, if not all, major industrial societies have a national health insurance plan, except the richest of all, America. The fact that we do not is another symptom of economic despotism. How much unnecessary suffering do we have to have in the United States so that we can protect the world from the big bad rogue nations? Or is this just an excuse that is a convenient argument to spend our surplus supporting the military industrial complex? Whatever the reason that we are unwilling to protect our citizenry from the economic and physical disaster of illness, it is a disgrace and outrage. There is never any shortage of apologists for greed, the palace guard of economic despotism. Some of the pompous potentates of punditry in the media have been doing a good job fooling the people for a long time now, and are making big bucks and big ego points for themselves in the process. They have been very successful in lazar lobotomizing into instant laughing hyenas the liberal establishment. Obviously, this would not be happening if the liberals were not vulnerable. Again, I believe the liberal vulnerability comes not so much from their ideology, as it does from the obsolescence of the system they must defend and can't. The worst of this detracting cult of bad mouthing scoundrels are the talk radio and cable TV news show hosts. They are the sophists of our time. (Sophists were paid public speakers of ancient Athens) They are dishonest or stupid ignoramuses fooling people by cleverly appealing to their worst sides with asinine gallows humor, outright lies, cheap rhetorical tricks and stupid egregious distortions of the truth. Some of the most prominent examples are Shaun Hannity, Rush Limbaugh and writer big mouth Ann Coulter. These vermin were berated in ancient Athens for ruining democracy and they are damaging it now by spreading lies and confusion and appealing to man's worst side. And all of us, if we do not reject the bad ideas of these whores and pimp sell outs to the masters of greed, are going to inherit the white tornado. Or have we already?

It is high time we stopped passing the buck to future generations and started solving problems now. This aforementioned self-development triad should be a part of the constitution of any free democratic country and should be added to the Bill of Rights of the American Constitution. Without the guarantee of a job, education, and health care, life in today's world of high prices is an immediate sentence of poverty and degradation. Only a pseudo democracy would consider anything less than this the bottom line of equality. The next generation of social systems must make sure that the words of democracy are in sync with the deeds performed for the people. Today, all we get are words. The addition of this triad of self-development to a capitalist economic system would add most of the appealing aspects of genuine socialism to capitalism. It would also protect the capitalist system from the downturn of the business cycle that can threaten its very existence. Contrary to most economists' firm politically correct current belief that it can't happen again, you can bet there will be a major downturn in the business cycle again. The current high price of gold over 700 (early 06) per once is an indication that a lot of astute people may be trying to hedge against such an event at present. Unfortunately, it takes a crisis such as the great depression of the 1930's before problems are seriously addressed in

America. The economists are usually wrong, because they are for the most part paid to put on the masters of greed's happy face.

None of this proposed triad of democratic rights is feasible as long as they must be factored into the price of non-parity competition, as they must be. This is why these things, even if proposed in congress, have not been enacted or taken seriously because they will only, under present world economic reality, have the effect of terminally damaging American companies ability to compete. If we want genuine democracy in America, we must be able to compete to pay for it. Parity can make this happen by making possible the fabled "level playing field" we have heard so much talk of. If there is another way that isn't hot air demagoguery, I would like to hear about it. We cannot build democracy by adding these things to our debt as some politicians glibly propose.

That we have not seen fit to allow our democracy to evolve to encompass these important issues is the most damning example of the lack of concern of politicians for the well being of their constituents that can possibly be imagined. Let's call a spade a spade. If you don't care whether your constituents have a job, if you don't care if they have an education to get a good job or if you don't care if they can obtain medical care when needed, what do you care about? Not these things obviously. Do any of you ask yourself this question when you vote? Unless you are rich enough to not give a damn about your neighbor, why do you vote at all? Your vote is denying these things to your neighbor and yourself. Of course, this may also be your intention. This is just an indication or symptom of the dangerous loss of moral compass that happens when a capitalist controlled economic system is allowed to dominate the political process without even a whimper of protest from the corporate conglomerate owned media. Their bottom line is in a different place than the one is that would bring about human happiness, which is not one of their profit streams. And that is now the reality in America. We are a corporate dictatorship, which is defined as corporations controlling a majority of congress paid for by campaign contribution bribes. We can call ourselves a democracy, a republic, or a ham sandwich, but the fact is we are a corporate state and I doubt whether it will make much difference which party is in office. As long as corporations have the right to bribe officeholders, they will continue to dictate how politicians vote. If he flies on corporate jets like a duck; if he quacks for globalization like a duck; if he votes for free trade like a duck; if he votes for bills written by corporate lobbyists like a duck, you can bet he's a duck. If you want to have real democracy, get rid of these lame ass ducks and take back the government from corporate control.

Chapter 9.

An Ideal Democracy,

Some Modest Ideas For a Better World

"If you would not be forgotten, as soon as you are rotten, either write things worth reading or do things worth writing."

Benjamin Franklin

"Down With the Minimum Wage, Up With the Maximum Wage."

Ed Wode

It makes little difference in today's world whether you have a country like the United States with 500 + large socialist like corporations that have the government in their back pocket, (An indirect corporate dictatorship) or a country like communist China, with one socialist dictatorship government (Socialist in name only, really capitalist) encompassing 500 + socialistic capitalist corporations, the world is going to be run by bureaucracy and socialism for rich corporations. It is just a question of whether we the people are going to have any say in our economic destiny or the converse as things pretty much are now. If we can harness the power of the sun and the atom, we can harness the power of corporate gigantism. It is just a question of the will of the people being harnessed. Domestication of this procrustean animal will make possible a human renewal that will truly revolutionize mass values and lifestyles. Toward this end, however, all the misunderstood ambiguities of "who represents who" must be done away with. We the people must be unequivocally represented by people who really represent the people, if that is constitutionally possible. The power of corporations must be in some way humanized and democratized by effective opposing power. In the U.S., the corporations and their running dogs in and out of government, must be checked by an effective individualist opposition that can only be permanently effective if it modifies the basically weak structure of government by making appropriate amendments to the Constitution. The world is now under the domination of corporate entities that will not give up power unless people fight for it.

The American people should wake up and realize that we are living in a past that was not all that good anyway. The despots of capitalism are not going to give up their divine right to dictate our choices, without a fight. Not being challenged enough by opposing politicians to be concerned that their system is in danger, because of their success in deluding the people into a state of false security, they will continue to starve the goose that lays the golden egg of its share of the pie until the people resolutely take what is rightfully theirs. The Federal Reserve knows what is best for the economy. According to former head Mr. Alan Greenspan, there is an optimal amount of employment and unemployment. Just enough to prevent job earnings inflation. They just announced today, the ides of March 06 that job growth is excellent; nothing about the kind of jobs. To me, this is dishonest. And the stupid corrupt media will let them get away with it. We seem to prefer floating in an economic-social-political limbo bordering on the hysterical, rather than to attempt to seriously solve our problems. The masters of greed prefer to have just enough unemployment to bring pressure on workers to work for the lowest possible wages. This unethical concept of capitalist economics should be rejected and replaced by a higher principle that everyone has a right to a good paying life-fulfilling job.

The failure to interpolate the current job quality meltdown, as a crisis is the worst failure of all. Corporations and the men who run them should come to grips with the reality that they are part of an organic machine in which the whole is only as good as the sum of the parts. The more people can earn the more they can buy. The more they can buy, the more demand there is for goods and services. The more successful people are, the more business benefits. Everyone, except anti-consumerists, knows and accepts this simple truth. No one, however, wants to take the responsibility to see that there is an investment in people that is as well planned and profitable as is investing in the supply side of the equation, which is the capitalist production part. The problem is that the corporation, the capitalist and the government are all cheating on the taxpayer and not just the other way around. Cheating is one of the most popular human games and we really ought to have a game by that name, if we don't already. It would be a sort of Monopoly for budding white-collar thieves. You could play a piece such as a government employee waiting to retire and go to work as an employee of the company he used to be paid to regulate or a CEO getting an obscene salary for pumping up the companies stock by hook or crook or a politician getting golf trips or other bribes from that same CEO or a lobbyist bribing congress people with campaign contributions or a Senator or president's son getting away with flagrantly obvious insider trading or a VP using influence to start wars that help your old company get no-bid contracts or defense secretaries making millions on the stock of a pharmaceutical company selling worthless virus medicines against bird flu, or house majority leaders that get away with taking lobbyist bribes that his predecessor just resigned for taking or oh the possibilities are almost endless. The capitalist dominated neo-conservative government we recently had clearly did not consider itself responsible for investing in people, because Republicans do not think government has a role in empowering people or doing much of anything else constructive for that matter. Let's hope the new conservative Democrats do not have the same attitude about people investing, but don't hold your breath. * "People are expendable and easily replaced by immigrants who will work for less and complain less, so why bother about them. Thank God for ubiquitous contraceptives and homos or we would be drowning in complainers." * That's a quote from the mind of the smart money. Meanwhile, the continuity of our culture goes down the drain. Even with the unbelievable amount spent on education, we must import a large percentage of our high-end skilled workers, because there is something drastically wrong with our education methods. We need to emulate more successful education systems in other countries like Japan.

Man makes social progress by reforms. The reformist movement when successful becomes part of the establishment and then part of the problem. That is why strong reformist movements are going to be necessary until we learn how to create heaven on earth. As it says in the Bible, there is a battle going on between the sons of light and the sons of darkness. Unfortunately, because of the ambiguity of religion, it is difficult to distinguish between the two sometimes; everyone claims he is on God's side except for Bush who claims God is on his side. I don't think so. Only the devil is capable of making more of a mess than Bush has. That is why we should not listen to those who mix politics and religion. God is on the side of everyone with good intentions, but only true democracy can create an unambiguous plan for heaven on earth. The majority of our politicians have sold their souls to the predatory sons of darkness and we are paying a terrible price. We must do something about this. Campaign finance reform is the only thing that can take back the government. Special interest campaign donations must be entirely cut off, union as well as corporation. We must revolutionize this struggle against special interest with renewed down to earth laws prohibiting this campaign bribery.

Public financing is the way to solve this problem and democratize running for office. It is very successful in several states. Big money defeated this initiative along with other important initiatives in California in the mid term o6. Those included a tax on the oil companies and one on cigarettes. The oil companies spent over 100 million to defeat this oil tax. "But we'll be bock!", said the govenator. By pretending to be a Democrat in his issue stands and spending 82 million to defeat the Democrat who had only half as much to spend, he won reelection handily. Many Hollywood stars supported him, taken in by high profile issues he initiated. Only a former actor like myself can appreciate the shallowness of most actors. The real Schwarzenegger is the one who vetoed a bill that would have cleaned up pollution in Long Beach, a city adjacent to Los Angeles with a population of 500 thousand, that is the most polluted place in the United States. A .30-cent tax on each container that arrives at the combined ports of L.A./Long Beach would have provided the funds to solve this problem. "Bod for business," said Arnold Schwarzenegger. I have one suggestion for initiative initiators. Have a budget big enough to fight your adversaries' lies on TV or don't waste your time. These aforementioned initiatives were drowned by big business money. The public campaign initiative seemed to have zero TV ads in the L.A. metropolitan area, whereas the opposition was ubiquitous. You can't win that way.

The Parity equality manifesto supports a strong central government, as necessary to coordinate and protect the important elements of society and make business realize it is just one important part of a living machine that has certain patriotic obligations to the society as a whole. Among the obligations assumed for the privilege of making money should be to not only provide security and healthy working conditions for workers, but all workers should be given a chance to participate in ownership in the company they work for through various stock incentives. People should have cradle to grave job security similar to the Japanese system. At least like that in Japan! (Nissan Motor Company has just announced they will no longer give health and pension benefits to American workers in America. The excuse is in order to remain globally competitive) This is fast becoming a mantra for degradation of jobs in developed countries. The French just tried to put in place a change of law stated to make their companies more competitive in the global market. Massive demonstrations by French students, who were the ones most effected, caused the scrapping of this law. This is the best example of why there is a need for Parity Economics. This law would have had the result of making French students subject to the hiring and firing whims of corporations based not on the need for employment of citizens, but on improving the bottom line of corporations at the expense of job security in France. Who says the frogs are dumb? This law was going to discriminate against French students who need jobs, but could be replaced by cheaper labor from outsourcing or immigration. The competitive global economy is necessitating these kinds of measures to try to level the playing field so that corporations can be globally competitive. However such measures cause discrimination against workers in developed countries who can't compete against the wages paid to third world workers. That is why the slogan of this book is down with minimum wage, up with maximum wage. Only a Parity system can make possible the leveling of the economic playing field without turning everyone into coolies. All kinds of discrimination must be eliminated. People should get equal pay for equal work the world over. But, not by being reduced to the lowest common denominator. This kind of globalization must be banned.

Foreign investment by American companies should be scrutinized as to whether the use of capital overseas will take jobs away from American workers. I think it should be incumbent on any investment over a certain amount to show whether that capital and/or technology is going to be used to compete for American jobs. If a mutual benefit is claimed, it should be proven. As harsh as this sounds, the Chinese just announced April 06 that Chinese citizens could for the first time make small overseas investments. If we had such a law restraining small investment, China would not be growing so spectacularly, fueled in great part by American investors. I am not suggesting restraint on small foreign investments, but it might well have some validity for large corporate transfers of capital and technology. We should also not allow manufacturing plants to close, as they are now doing all over the country, without the government looking at the possibility of them either staying open or being converted to other similar uses. I am not trying to be dogmatic in these ideas, but I do think that the government should have more to say in the movement of capital and technology abroad that effects American jobs. The problem is, can government do anything right? Not much it seems. Government is there to be used as more than a hardhat rack, contrary to what those who have sold their souls to the corporations would have us believe. We need to make it competent. Capital and tech is the heart of any economy. It seems Boeing, which has paid several fines for illegal transfers of technology, pays no attention to laws affecting such dangerous transfers. The Chinese have understood the risk of this for millennia. It used to be a death penalty in China at the time of Marco Polo to transfer silk technology out of the country.

Almost any country can now come into America and raise money in the capital markets, so it may be a moot point I am raising here I admit. China has recently gone public to raise capital for its second largest bank and the offering was way oversubscribed. Next, they will do the same with their largest bank. Some of the investors are Americans. This is not the same as corporate transfers of capital and technology resulting in loss of jobs by Americans. If this is for no other reason than to increase the greedy bottom line of an American corporation, a stop should be put to it. Voters should have an awareness of the significance of what has been taking place to transfer the American economy overseas. If most of the promises of mutual benefits turn out to be a fraud, as it appears they are, how can the American voter, without some such historical perspective, make an intelligent choice when he goes to the polls? Has anyone challenged the perpetrators of these mutual job benefit claims that were made in order to prove or disprove those claims? Does anyone even remember those PR campaigns? I do.

We should also take a very hard look at military technology being shipped abroad. I think major condemnatory criticism of the military-industrial-government complex is the incredible amount of arms we have been shipping to the third world now and in the past. Certainly, this has backfired on us dangerously when the fair weather friends have turned foul, as with Iran, Afghanistan and now Venezuela. Some of the weapons we blunderingly supplied, including ground to air missiles to the Afghans fighting the Russians, are probably the geneses of the prestige earned by the current terrorists that are attacking us. This terrorist war must somehow be won quickly or it may well be the ruination of our country. Accepting the idea that this war will drag on for a long time may be the biggest mistake of an administration that is one big mistake. It's a cancer that will worsen until it destroys us. Bush, not concentrating on excising this tumor, may have planted the seeds of the destruction of our country. This man, Osama Bin Laden, has mobilized a vast nation of over one billion people in many countries to hate us. We must win this war soon before WMDs become readily available to these terrorists, as they will at some point. If we don't, they will sooner or later get them and destroy us with likely impunity. You better take this as a prophetic warning America. (I sound like the Colbert Report pseudo egotist, Steven Colbert) We must get rid of this pathetic bumbler Bush 2 and defeat these terrorists pronto even if it means mobilizing for a real war in America and putting us on a real world war footing. We cannot rely on Pakistan to do this job for us. They really are a big part of the problem. We must go where this rat is holed up and exterminate him and his followers, whatever the consequences. This cancer must be stamped out by all means. As for Bush's doctrine of pre-emption, I agree with it. Contrary to those who say this is too macho and illegal of Bush, I think it is not macho enough. It is not enough to present it as an "on the table" verbal threat. Threats do not inhibit our present adversaries. They look at it as hot air rhetoric, which it is along with the rest of Bush's public pronouncements. We must unequivocally give these rogue nations an ultimatum to stop their WMD development within a definite deadline or face annihilation. Anything short of this kind of threat is no threat at all. A good idea doth not a mushroom cloud maketh. It takes a bunker buster nuke. There's a little culture for you. That's why I look at Bush as short of the mark on this issue as on everything else. The time for idle threats and bluffing is over. These opponents must know we mean business. If we don't stop this proliferation, our country is going to be destroyed. We are in WW III, make no mistake about it. To win, we must win while we have the unmistakable overwhelming advantage. This window of opportunity is shrinking fast.

America's arms economy has proliferated to the point that it could be said that the business of America is no longer business but arms. And we are now paying a dear price for this immoral behavior. It does not take a rocket engineer to see why we are spending an inordinate amount of our taxes on arms. Arms production has become synonymous with big business. The main symptom of the arms plague that has infected America is that sometimes our latest military equipment is offered and has been sold abroad before our own military has these weapons. This means we have to constantly upgrade our technology to stay ahead not only of our adversaries, but also of ourselves, if we want to have a tech advantage. The billions thus wasted could finance a health care system and education and much more that is needed. America is the laughing stock of the world in many ways and this is one of them.

Obviously, the cynical men who are the real power behind the throne in America do not feel it is of consequence that our military technology becomes obsolete as fast as we spend billions of tax dollars to develop it. It is said that the Mongol warriors who conquered the widest expanse of territory in history, including China, most of Russia, the Middle East and part of Europe were invincible because they had the first cavalry in history with stirrups that allowed soldiers to fire arrows with accuracy. Heat-seeking missiles allowed us to attain air superiority in the Korean War after initially being at a disadvantage to Russian planes that had better close combat firepower and pilot training. Any small tech edge in war is enough to spell the difference between victory and defeat. We narrowly averted disaster in Korea because of this stupid military blunder. We can never afford to become technologically behind militarily, but this does not mean we have to bankrupt ourselves on obsolete conventional or strategic weapon overkill. However, we are now in serious danger of this happening because of the erosion of our industrial base. Sony Corp. of Japan first made some of the smart bombs we like to brag about possible. Now, China has missile guidance technology supplied to them for satellite launching by American companies. I'm not a rocket scientist, but when one of their rockets lands on my house, I'm not going to be very surprised. I was surprised when I heard the Chinese owned a large shipping terminal in Long Beach where they unload their container ships. (This was long before the current ports controversy) One nuke in a shipping container and goodbye Long Beach. Of course, if it were to be planted by Al Qaeda, goodbye the U.S. and China, as they would both be conned into thinking the other was responsible. This is why this terrorist madness must come to an end soon or the world may. Most of the new electronic tech is coming from communist China. If they decide to become a serious adversary, we are in deep poo.

It is clear that the real masters of America at the moment are the hucksters of greed who will do anything for a buck. This patriotism for a buck is what corporations best exemplify. Any time patriotism is a moneymaker, you quickly see flag-waving P.R. commercials bragging about how much is being done for the cause of freedom. As mentioned, one of the most obscenely brazen P.R. commercial campaigns that ran for years was the one that claimed exporting American jobs abroad would create a balanced two-way trade beneficial in jobs to both countries. The end result has been this whole outsourcing tidal wave we now have. It is certainly true there are benefits in trade, but at this point it appears to be corporate executives getting obscene salaries, rather than American workers, who are benefiting. It remains to be seen how this is going to play out.

Why is it that so much of our economy, especially products that we have always excelled in, is no longer manufactured in America? We the people should be the ones who have the final say in what is good for us, not some corporate executive interested only in maximizing profits for his corporation. This corporate greed not only affects worker paychecks, but it stymies entrepreneurial individualism. How can the great American individualist make a contribution in the manufacturing sector, when there is practically no sector left? He can't, because he can't compete with global corporatist socialism doing business where the workers can be exploited to the slave like maximum. This is why Parity equality reform is imperative if we wish to restore a real market economy based on individualist capitalist freedom.

Parity stands for a gradual return to a peacetime economy by all countries for the first time since W.W. II. The level of arms production is such that it probably is one of the main factors contributing in what seems to be endless wars. One American Secretary of State made the crack " Why have such a terrific military if we aren't going to use it". The Bush W. Iraq war may be a case in point answering this question. Was Rumsfeld playing with the toys, because he could? The arms proliferation has no doubt been a profit center for many American companies and most states to some degree. The B2 bomber has parts that are made in all 50 states. This is a form of military pork that increases the cost of production unnecessarily. It is also a form of defense department lobbying for votes from the state's congressional representatives. Military spending, when proper, is also a form of valuable job creating public works for America, when it hasn't been out of control, as in the Vietnam War when it may have been a cause of inflation. There is the question of whether we can handle a shift to a peacetime economy without serious danger to national security as well as the economy. This impacts not only jobs. Defense contractor's factories must be available viable entities when they are needed. Perhaps the government should consider keeping these factories available even when they are not needed. That might be a lot cheaper than keeping production going just to keep the factory from closing. An important lesson to be learned from these arms created jobs is that the government can and does act as a counterbalancing force when it creates economy, as it does with arms, space and other expenditures. Why, if the government can create jobs by spending hundreds of billions on arms, cannot government create better and more moral jobs by spending money to create jobs in peacetime pursuits? The answer to this hypothetical question is that it could if we did not have such a strong prejudice against government competition with private enterprise in America. This is a stupid mental cul de sac prejudice against government. Whereas private enterprise has limitations on the risks they can take, by risking taxpayer funds, government can afford to risk virtually unlimited funds and if it all went down the drain, which it would not, we would still be no worse off than we are by throwing our money permanently down the arms toilet. Underwriting private entities to actually operate these creatures of the government until they are profitable enough to be completely privatized could do this. Government would then be reimbursed for its investment and be able to use the funds again. It is clear that government can function as such a pump primer and counterbalancing force for the economy if it makes sense. There is currently a plan for the government to jump-start invest in starting some pharmaceutical companies to create vaccines that are needed to protect the nation against a pandemic. This is a good idea: one of the best in a long time. The fact that we will not actively pursue such a course under normal conditions is the result of us giving in to hysterical paranoia spread by big money. Afraid of competition, it claims that government will turn into socialism if it gets into business in a serious way. This is the pot calling the kettle black. We the people, if we want a free creative lifestyle, cannot, as we do now, allow ourselves, to be virtually dictated to by the oligarchs with the big money, because their perceived needs and our real needs are in conflict. Big money socialism for the rich cannot sleep at night for fear of socialism for little people. Those with big money are so frightened of socialism, except socialism for the rich, that they would rather see the country go down the drain than for us to have one more job that is not of their making. They will get their wish if things keep going the way they are. It is not in the interest of the people to have our government run by fear of socialism. Perhaps the post office should be turned into a private enterprise. We will have to pay for postage whether it is a private or public enterprise. And the post office is automating just like private enterprise. We should be flexible about our economy and what best serves the people. If savings and loans go belly up because of poor management, we the people should run them ourselves until the problem is fixed. If the government starts a maggot farm and maggots turn out to be a product that creates new jobs and is economically feasible, as soon as economically sensible, let private enterprise take over the government owned maggot business and the government can use the money it is paid to start another risky business ad infinitum. The Chinese have learned this lesson as they are buying and selling state owned businesses whenever it makes sense.

There are good reasons government should not try to do everything. Khrushchev once said, I believe less than tongue in cheek, "We are glad there is free enterprise capitalism in the West, because otherwise we would not know what to charge for our products". International competition, if it exists on a fair basis, will give a true market value for goods produced. Fair competition is the only way fair prices can be determined. Unfortunately fair competition does not always exist and it is therefore questionable whether there are fair prices at all at the present time. Certainly, based on the earnings of workers involved in global trade, most of them are being unfairly exploited. They should be paid much more and therefore prices for the goods they produce should be higher. As Khrushchev pointed out, socialist countries have no other way than a capitalist free market to determine the value of the goods that are produced. This is one of the fallacies that make pure monopoly socialism as obsolete and ineffective as pure capitalism. The fallacies of capitalism and socialism alone, as pointed out in this book, should make any open-minded person realize that we must have a new economic model based on correcting the errors of both ideologies. And I am sure serious students of economics could come up with many other serious defects of these systems. Government allowing the decentralization of its economy into socialistic corporatism is what we now call capitalist free enterprise, but it is really decentralized socialist planned enterprise. This decentralization of government is highly desirable, because too much centralization of power turns into a jungle of inefficient bureaucratization that tends to stifle human initiative and creativeness. There is just no way that man can more efficiently and creatively manage most business than by decentralized private management. But today, with billions of people to be looked after, some projects do require bureaucratization on a scale beyond the resources of private enterprise. The great problem that has to be soon resolved, if we are to evolve peacefully to the future, is how to resolve the present enmity between those who believe private initiative is the only way to do things and those who think government is the only way. There are quite obviously times when each is the best. We the people have to take the attitude that we do not care who does the job for us as long as the job of sustaining us gets done by the best possible means without pre-empting our personal right to freedom and privacy. If we do not resolve the unnecessary capitalist and socialist dichotomy intelligently and establish democracy under whatever ism, we have a very bleak future. There is a kind of truce between the two systems today that will hopefully end in a merger of the two. They are both faced with a new threat from a terrorism that will, if not stopped, turn the clock back to a time when man cannot solve the problems that must be solved soon. The very survival of the human race is on the line. The sun is dimming in more ways than one.

We cannot continue spending the world's surplus on worthless arms and hope to be able to deal with the problems of a world that is increasing in population more like a plague of locust than human beings. We are running out of all kinds of resources. If we do not first eat ourselves out of existence, we will clearly ruinously reduce the amount of air we have to breathe by deforestation or destroy the upper atmosphere from hot house gases or dim the sun from pollutants or flood our coasts and change our climate from global warming or run out of fresh water or run out of energy and on and on. We are at the same time eating up and killing off all the other species on land, sea and in the air. Our technology is dangerously out of control too. One deranged person can now be a threat to every living being on the planet through the genetic manipulation of disease genes or the food we eat. We are changing the climate so radically we are heading for either another ice age or higher temperatures that will result in flooded coastlines or that will turn much of the earth into desert waste. Fresh water, too, is running out and this threatens to turn much of the fertile belt in the United States and other places into desert waste. We are bordering on many crises because of excessive population and faulty consumer and industrial practices. Not for a minute longer can we ignore these problems without risking utter, irreversible, catastrophe. Mankind must renounce warfare as a solution to problems or we can never solve these other great problems.

We are within sight of the possibility of creating almost unlimited wealth through technology that will make possible utopian societies in which everyone can lead the good life in perfect health, fully educated and probably live to at least an enjoyable 100+. If we can find ways of limiting our longevity from cell damage and gene limiting factors, we have the possibility of creating virtual eternal life. If this seems ridiculous, as it does, consider that some turtles live to be 250 and some tree species over two thousand years. As we can share all genes with all other living things, anything they can do we can do better, as the saying goes. Whether this manipulation of nature is a good idea is another question. It is certainly fraught with dangers of mistakes or misuse.

All of this progress and potential progress will go down the drain if there is a WMD holocaust. And it is doubtful, because we will lack energy, technology and trained brains, that life will ever again have the same opportunity on this resource depleted planet. Man might then be doomed to a science fiction reality: a race of indigents slowly becoming extinct due to a lack of renewable resources. Our resource situation on this planet is so desperate now, that one step backward or any serious stagnation of development is going to result in just such a science fiction reality. Man is truly at a crossroads. He must now make a choice for life or suicide. Choosing life means a worldwide reformation in which all forms of government not truly democratic must, if possible, be peacefully replaced and replaced by governments committed to a pragmatic, utopian future. We must ostracize tyranny from the planet earth once and for all time. We cannot go forward unless we "make love and not war", unless you like war in bed. If we continue to sow the seeds of hatred, nothing we achieve will be worth the price we will pay in blood and repression of human freedom. It is far better to be dead than fed like a dog. Man truly does not live by bread or cake alone. We are spiritual beings and we demand to be treated like spiritual beings. However, there is spiritual and there is spiritual. Many people who claim to be spiritual are pseudo spiritual and dangerous to true spirituality. There is no exclusivity to spiritual, because no one knows for sure what is absolute spirituality. Those who claim their brand of spirituality is absolute truth are absolutely stupid. They are corrupting the concept of God. God *only* knows what the absolute is. God or science has never revealed any absolute knowledge to mankind yet. All our knowledge is relative and for good reason. We have never proven, as a race, that we can be trusted with power. As the saying goes, power corrupts and absolute power corrupts absolutely. When some claim their brand of spirituality is the only truth and are intolerant of other's beliefs, you know they are liars and bullies, because there is no absolute truth. And liars create most of the hell on earth, because they are dangerous fools.

On the other hand, let us all become good sports for the first time in history, and have non-lethal ideological war to our hearts content. Yes, nothing can be more fun for us spiritual beings than argumentative differences of opinion. Intellectual war is probably the single greatest amusement of humanity excluding sex. To kill one another because of such activity, the way we are now doing is ultimate stupid self-flagellation, the bane of man. Our spiritual and intellectual adversaries are our best friends and closest kin. Yes, let us have true freedom of speech everywhere. Freedom of speech is our greatest sport. It is the sport of philosopher kings, who are the true kings of the human race. The true kings of the world are those who give their all in the non-coercive enlightenment of their fellow man. Any country that does not allow freedom of speech is a tyranny, and should be peacefully replaced or ostracized from the human community until it reforms itself. Our important international debates should reach all the people of the world on the same day, so world public opinion can have an opportunity to vent its wrath or pleasure with questions of global importance.

If we remove the specter of poverty from the world, most men would turn from the worship of mammon materialism to beauty, truth, goodness and other manifestations of the spirit. It is fear of poverty that makes the human race mean spirited. And the way life is organized today, that is a very real fear that needs to be assuaged if people are ever to be really free to be their better selves.

People must debate their problems in order to have any possibility of coming to grips with them. Only when the people of the world truly understand their problems can they take the steps necessary to resolve them. People can now be easily misled because freedom of speech is a double edged sword. Wherever there is freedom of speech, it is abused by some. People should be careful whose freedom of speech they favor. The sophist media speakers of the world, in the pay of the crooks, are paid to manipulate people's opinions with lies and distortions of the truth. They get away with it by telling people what they want to hear that usually panders to their dark side. Everyone has some dark side he or she needs to be careful to keep reined in. I know I do. If you don't self-edit sometimes, you may find yourself exercising someone else's agenda instead of your own. This leads to bad choices, sadly inimical to your own best interest. In America, it is imperative we start picking leaders who are more intelligent and more for the people's interest. We have been picking the opposite lately thanks in great part to these foul perverters of free speech, the modern day sophists.

Let us tolerate every country in the world to freely choose whatever economic-political-social system best suits that country, as long as it is true democracy. I sound like Henry Ford the first, who said, "I don't care what color we make Fords as long as it is black." Our present policy of trying to impose our flaky pseudo democratic ideology on others looks a lot like a policy of hypocrisy and bullyism due to the fact that our own system is so obviously flawed. Our present leaders cannot see this, because of their own dumb self-serving denial. The time is past, in spite of what seems to be modest successes on both sides of the ideological curtain, when any kind of colonization, even ideological or economic colonization, of one country by another is a good idea. That is why the present arms struggles are so stupid and pathetic. Ultimately, the people of every country are going to choose a democratic process that is much superior to anything that now exists. The state of the art of democracy is presently at about the level of the invention of the wheel. Hopefully, the invention of the personal computer, an event of equal importance to any in history, will change all that, if it hasn't already.

The tools necessary for people to unite and democratize the world are in place. When there is a full consciousness of the impending need for world reform, people will rebel against the inertia that now dominates. The U.N. that in many ways is ineffective now, even as a peacekeeper should be enabled to do a lot more than just go into a country and keep the peace. It should be able to completely renovate what we now call failed states. This means there should be a trained force that is empowered to completely set up a viable economic-political-social system with a government that has the means to be a successful real democracy. First however, we need to create an example of real democracy that can be emulated.

Most Americans, because the press, the schools, television, film and other media are very close to or associated with the dominant political class, are misinformed or ill informed on how far removed our American system has come from the equality, fraternity, freedom and justice that should be the hallmarks of democracy. The media and those with access to the media in America vomit up a constant stream of America is the best of all countries because it is the freest most democratic place in the world. There is no place much better than America now for some, but that is certainly not true for all. To try to give the impression that we are even remotely the best that we can be is a big denial of reality. There are many better places in some aspects now, such as higher per capita standard of living, longer life, more health benefits and other things, but taking the whole gamut of choices, I'll still take America. Some oil sheikdoms in the Middle East already bestow economic benefits matching and even surpassing my best proposals here, but when and if the oil runs out, they will probably revert to economic as well as political despotisms. Hopefully not. Maybe Bush's effort to transplant our pseudo democracy will somehow spread by some miracle. How free we really are is questionable. I would say we have more an illusion of freedom, as explained many times and many ways in this book, than real freedom. Real freedom is synonymous with real democracy.

The mentality of the American public in recent years of liberal floundering has been bent out of shape by a virtually one-way debate dominated by the Republicans. Criticism of our mounting problems has been countered with simplistic hot air solutions that for the most part have left government legislative action grid-locked except for a couple of scam like things. This has allowed the Rooseveltian renaissance to founder on Republican pie-in-the-sky shoals. Democrat timidity, while in power, to actually take the bold steps necessary to adequately advance democracy, has allowed the aristocrats of inaction to proclaim "do-nothing" as a religion, in spite of the fact that the people clearly want a remedy for the do-nothingness. This confusing situation resulting in a polarized legislative gridlock has been caused because the liberal democrats never really had a historic majority. This became apparent when the solid Democrat Party conservative South converted to become the solid Republican Party conservative south. Therefore, we are still being punished by the retarded part of the south for the civil war by being denied genuine democracy. The high priests of "do-nothing" have opportunistically taken advantage of the confusion to make "do nothing" seem like "do everything instantly" at one fell swoop. The ascension of this bunch in office now is a total disaster. As they ignore science in favor of political expediency, ignore economic reality to pander to global corporate interest that favors the economies of other countries, waste of our resources on unnecessary wars, radically infringing on our constitutional traditions with things such as: lie to the American people about national security to start wars; ignore the Geneva convention by using torture on captured prisoners; foment state subsidy of religious organizations that is constitutionally prohibited; ruin of our international reputation by ignoring treaties and other traditional cooperation with our allies; opposition to family planning in the third world; ignoring global warming initiatives and drastically endangering our national security by the dumb way they are doing things, this administration has created the biggest mess in our history.

The Katrina debacle was another symptom of the politically biased way the current administration is running things. And they have gotten away with murder because no one has told it like it is. I firmly believe New Orleans' destruction should be directly attributable to politically expedient hanky-panky. Louisiana had a Democrat governor and New Orleans a black Democrat mayor. What better way to get rid of this Democrat enclave in a solid Republican South than to make these politicians look bad. The rest of you may have fallen off a turnip truck on your heads, but I haven't. This is SOP smear treatment to politically unfriendly places and people by this vicious administration. Bush recently (4/06) turned down Gov. Schwarzenegger for funds to repair our aging and vulnerable levees here in Ca. even though the Govenator is a Republican. They're setting us up for the same kind of fall as New Orleans for the same reason. This is a solidly democratic state unlikely to elect Republicans unless they are a star like Schwarzenegger. Trying to sell our vulnerable port management to an Arab owned company in the midst of the wake from 9/11 shows how insensitively contemptuous of the public they are. Even though this deal has been squashed, it exposes just how fanatically dumb or corrupt their public interest priorities really are. Global wheeling and dealing is more important to them than the American people's security. Just as attempting to win the hearts and minds of Iraqis for the oil industry has been a more important priority than winning the war and saving the lives of American soldiers. Also, what has not dawned on the pundit media geniuses yet is that we are almost back to the cold war with Russia over the oil in former Soviet states in central Asia. The big clue to the clueless here is that V.P. Cheny (5/4/06) is leading the verbal attack on trying to intimidate Russia. He doesn't mention this dogfight over oil of course, but criticizes Russia for everything else. Everyone is wondering why. The wolf wants to eat the oil stupid. We are playing a dangerous political game with Russia that started in Clinton's administration. To me the worst blunder in America's diplomatic history up to that time was favoring the Poles and other Eastern Europeans over the Russians after a sea change political-economic conversion of Russia and all for short-term domestic political gain. What good has it done us to provoke the Russians by adding these countries to NATO? Are they going to protect us from Russian missiles? This policy was as stupid as anything Bush has done. We don't understand diplomacy in America and have converted it into a wrecking ball wielded by inept, corrupt or stupid often redneck politicians, mostly all three at once. Are we due for a rude awakening or not? Wake up American people! Your leaders are throwing dice with your lives.

The Parity equality manifesto proclaims that a new constitutional convention should be called for the purpose of modernizing and challenging the merits of the present form of government and changing it where needed. This is a constitutionally legal, but difficult and virtually impossible course to take. It is authorized by article V of the constitution, only if article V is allowed to be amended first:

"Unless Article V is amended first to allow it, a Convention for Proposing

Amendments can never become a true constitutional convention, i.e., it can never

write a new constitution. And neither can Congress".

What is recommended in the constitution short of a constitutional convention per se is a "convention for proposing Amendments …as part of the Constitution". Therefore, amendments in mass can be proposed in such a non-constitutional convention. That is what I am recommending. Not totally rewriting the constitution, which is prohibited unless there is an amendment of article V. Even to bring this "Convention for Proposing Amendments" about is well neigh impossible, however, considering that the rules for enacting it are the votes for of three fifths of state's legislatures. Admittedly, all of this is highly unlikely unless there is uniform desperation throughout the union. We may yet see this. Short of this, perhaps a mock constitutional convention should be held to simulate as an example what improvements could be built into a new constitution. We do not pretend here to have all the answers as to what should be done to fix our muscle-bound gridlocked government, but like Paul Revere sounding the alarm, I for one, am convinced it is a disaster,

Certainly the presidential part of the government is obsolete. It's a virtual 8 year limited dictatorship or monarchy, as interpreted by its present occupant who blatantly ignores laws as he chooses.

It is always a wonder to me that when people vote for the promises of a candidate that are not kept, in order to punish the reneging fraud, they vote next election for what is the only other alternative offered, who usually also makes promises he can't keep, and then when he disappoints them, they go back and vote for the party they had voted out of office for not keeping its promises in the first place, and on and on ad infinitum. There must be some way out of this vicious circle of bad choices. I for one took Gore Vidal's advice and dropped out of voting for a long time. This is a bad idea though and I have since returned to the fold. Sometimes judicious voting does make a difference. At present, there is no other way of rewarding or punishing candidates and putting them out of office can punish at least terrible politicians and parties. But it doesn't change much in the big picture. Only fundamental changes of the system, such as some of the ones proposed here, could produce big changes like ones that are needed now.

I wonder if we shouldn't seriously consider taking away a President's pension and P.X. privileges if he does not keep a high percentage of his promises or have a very good reason why he does not. Perhaps if he does not keep a reasonable percentage of his promises we should have a mechanism for a recall vote to put him or her out of office. It certainly would not be the end of the world to put a crooked or incompetent President out of office, as Jerry Ford replacing Nixon proved. At present, Presidents are virtually untouchable except for impeachment that is very difficult. People were saying how honest Reagan seemed, when right after his election, in one of his first off-the-cuff cracks to a reporter's question, he admitted that one of the things he said while campaigning was "just campaign rhetoric." (A euphemism for lying) We have become so jaded about being lied to by politicians that a newly elected President can make such a disclosure without raising an eyebrow. Therefore, one of the first qualifications for getting elected President of the United States is to be a consummate liar.

It is a sad commentary on the presidential system that voters often vote more against the loser than they do for the winner. I think in Reagan's case, he as architect of the misnamed conservative agenda we are still suffering under mobilized a following of people fearful that Carter's human rights stand was weakness at the same time that Carter was extremely unpopular with virtually everyone because of the Iran hostage mess. Many people who did vote for Carter may have done so more out of a prudent fear of Reagan's macho ideas than out of any love of Carter, who was destroyed by allowing himself to appear to be weak to a degree detrimental to the macho reputation of the country. He appeared to be obsessed with, but unwilling, if necessary, to take decisive action to solve the Iran hostage problem. The democrats still carry this weak on security baggage. Carter was really not much different than all the presidents from Truman through Ford. All of these Presidents acted more in a caretaker role, encouraging mild evolvement of the democratic

system, as opposed to being strong ramrod reformists like Roosevelt.
Reagan represented the first true extreme that occupied the presidency
since Roosevelt. Even Nixon, sans Watergate, would have been
known as a moderate.

We are now at a historic crossroad when the present administration
is under attack from many directions and doesn't seem to know how
to respond except to spin a bunch of lies to the public that everything
is going fine. We are in danger of losing our entire manufacturing
base, bogged down in at least three wars, in an outsourcing of jobs
stampede and they have the balls to spin us that everything is great
because the stock market is doing well. We need a strong reformist
leader like Wilson or Roosevelt who will tell us the truth and ram
through the appropriate remedial legislation to put us back on the right
track or we are going to be up the proverbial creek without the
proverbial paddle. As I don't think that will happen under the present
two parties, I would rather see a new third party lead the way. And
Franklin D. Roosevelt's ideas for an economic bill of rights would be
a good place to start amending the constitution. He certainly realized
that our current form of government left a lot to be desired or he
would not have made revolutionary proposals such as his Economic

Bill of Rights. What better authority for change could there be? This was a serious proposal. But we don't do serious political change in America. We do sports, drink Bud, piss a lot and auto-genocide ourselves on birth control devices. The result: 500,000 Mexicans waving Mexican flags marching through downtown Los Angeles trying to blackmail us into capitulating to their illegal immigration demands. Will we? You bet! It cost the GOP the 06-midterm election. The rest is hot air. Fodder for the news talk junkies.

And whom are we voting for when we vote for President? This is another sad commentary. We do not know who the man really is, what he really stands for, or what his M.O. is going to be until after he takes office and it is too late. We vote almost entirely for an image that has been created by professional advertising people and speechwriters and have little or no idea of whether the man is bona fide or a writer's alter ego. Who specifically is best qualified to be President of the United States? My answer to that one is probably no one is truly qualified to be President of the United States because it is an outmoded way to rule. It has become tantamount to electing a dictator or monarch for four years in the sense that, for all practical purposes it is impossible to remove him if he is incompetent. If I had to make a choice, under the present deplorable system, I would say that presidential candidates should be limited to black women, particularly those who have lived all their lives in the slum ghettos of America and have fought to raise a large family against every conceivable hardship that exists to make life hell on earth. Someone with that background of suffering would not know any better than to have the compassion and determination to genuinely attack the problems confronting this country. The Presidency of the United States is the most obsolete part of an obsolete system. Once a candidate has successfully gone through the grueling process to run for president that now takes years of campaigning, if he wins he has to "land running" with a plan to save a country, the problems of which have been compounding for years and even decades. If his plan does not show very positive almost immediate effect or if his policies are unpopular, he will probably be voted out of office after his first term. This means that the President spends a great deal of energy catering to public taste and often makes decisions that are popular as opposed to what is in the national interest. Another absurdity of our governing method is the President often has to face a hostile Congress controlled by another party and must spend a great deal of time and energy pleading, compromising and selling out to get any program through.

Even a President whose own party controls Congress can have a rough time, as Bush is at present May 06, thank God. It sounds contradictory to say the president has to cater to congress when I have characterized the office as a dictatorship, but this is the essence of pseudo democracy: defined as doing the opposite of what public opinion polls say people want with the full support of a congress controlled by corporations and other special interests. His job description should be snowing the gullible people of America that he represents them instead of his true corporate masters.

Sometimes politicians of the same party are actually of opposite political poles philosophically. This was the case for years in the solid Democrat south that was really the solid conservative south that pulled its weight toward preventing a liberal agenda from coming to fruition. In practice, this was mainly a strategy to prevent black Americans from having their full civil rights. Rebelling against a single piece of legislation, which goes against the grain of one's conscience is one thing. But blocking the agenda of your party for decades as the southern Democrats did was destructively obscene. The liberal democrats were never able to realize their agenda because of this, which has been a disaster for democracy in America. Of course, the difference between Democrats and Republicans is usually more blurred than it is now with a man of an extremely unorthodox, if not a radical agenda in the oval office. This example brings to mind the whole Republican Party agenda that considers people needs secondary to the interests of business. Even though there is a great polarization in the rhetorical beliefs of Democrats and Republicans at present, some of the Democrats also are representing corporate interests more than those of the people. The difference between the two parties in some cases, but not all, is more one of style than of substance.

Our system of allowing Senators and Representatives to be bribed by special interests giving campaign contributions, paying hefty speech honorariums and giving other donated perks is a corrupting fiasco, and must be changed if government is ever to become an effective tool for creating a people concerned democracy. The parliamentary system, although no panacea per se, eliminates much of the unnecessary duplicity of our system of catatonic protocols, most of which are used more for obstruction of good legislation then for constructive purposes. And it eliminates the President entirely, which is O.K. with me. Let the pros do the job. At least when they mess up, they usually do not have the excuse of inexperience. It might be possible to work out a compromise system between our system and a parliamentary system. An idea along this line is the following: irrespective of whether a leader is elected by the people or the Congress, the man, elected should always be supported by a majority philosophically committed to back his program. He should then be able to pass the programs he has promised without delay or compromise. Nothing is more ridiculous about the American system than that we elect men to office who must fight tooth and nail to have their program put into operation. The concept of checks and balances has too often turned into checkmate period. Most legislation in the U. S. ends up compromised to the point that it is not very effective. Whether good or bad, the American people deserve to get what they have mandated. Anything short of this just creates confusion, and that is one of the main reasons the people of America are now confused and frustrated. However, in order for this to be a valid mandate, the candidate's agenda should be published in writing during his presidential campaign in a simple form understandable to people. This way, people are able to vote as much for the candidate's agenda, as they do for the candidate. What could be more common sensible than this? Rudy Giuliani in his 08 presidential primary campaign has a list.

The beginning of the end for ancient Greek democracy was a greed motivated attack on the Sicilian city-state of Syracuse, ironically a Greek colony. Athens lost the flower of its youth in this attack and all but the rich of its captured soldiers, who could afford to have themselves ransomed, spent the rest of their days as slaves in the quarries of Sicily. The descendent genes of some of these unfortunate men, if they were ever released in place, may be among the present day Mafiosi. Democracy, as in the case of ancient Athens, is no guarantee against despotism and military adventurism. Just because the majority decides to enslave his fellow man does not make that man any less of a slave or the democrats any less the despots.

Perhaps a President should be elected for a period that would be limited by his popularity. When every voter has a home computer terminal to vote this will be a practical possibility without costing an excessive amount of money. Then there could be a mechanism for a regular recall vote of confidence to be held often, perhaps as often as every one or two years to see if he is still wanted. This way we can close the circle and have real *direct* democracy for the first time since ancient Athens. If it were desirable, there could be votes on all national issues, every issue if need be. Computers have made everything possible. This kind of direct democracy will happen eventually. Probably even a world government will come about in the future. Who knows what surprises the future holds? One thing we know for sure; things will not stay the same forever, because forever is the future. And that's a long time. One of the best pieces of advice I was ever given that has saved me from plenty of grief when I have followed it, is that you should always have a back door to go through if you make a bad mistake. In life, which is never perfect, you should always carry a parachute. Why should this principle not apply when the life of the republic is in the hands of one person?

Another idea appropriate for any democratic government, whether our present form or parliamentary, is that instead of risky public campaigning, (That is no longer the most effective way to campaign anyway) we should exclusively have television debate, and advertising paid for by public financing; the money for this should be raised by a special tax on corporations. Direct corporate funding of elections should be banned entirely. Public live campaigning is obsolete. Public live campaigning is just an excuse to divide and conquer the public; an excuse to tell different constituencies different things based on what they want to hear and this often is, the opposite of what the candidate said to another group the day before. Amid the current immigration controversy, I just saw a campaign picture of George W. Bush marching down the street with a Latina, carrying the Mexican flag and singing the national anthem in Spanish. I don't know whether this was a hoax picture or not, but there's the classic example of the ends a politician will go to get elected. We must elect people to our highest public offices that are statespersons representing all the people, and not political hacks trying to represent special interests or be everything to everybody and then end up being nothing to nobody. I think limiting campaigning to television debate would produce much higher quality candidates and do away with a lot of campaign rhetoric because this would force each candidate to really be up on his "p's" and "q's". Debate speech should be spontaneous and just as much a surprise to the speaker as to the audience. No advance questions to study should be allowed. In this way we would have a much truer portrait of whom the man we are voting for really is and the nimbleness of his wits.

There is a way - of this you can he certain - of vastly improving our antiquated system, but first we have to get over the silly sentimentality that we have the best of all possible governments and realize that our system is dangerously obsolete. Our forebears were wise and well educated for the task they took on, but they did not have a crystal ball and, therefore, could not look into the future and see how different our world would be from theirs of two hundred years ago. Our Constitution was written in horse and buggy days and is, in fact, a horse and buggy constitution compared to what it should be. Two hundred years ago there was little or no experience with democracy and the problems it might incur, because there was only Greece and Rome from ancient history as an example. Things have not changed much have they? Rome's republican government was overthrown for a lot of the same reasons we are having political troubles in twenty-first century America. The republic was overthrown from within because public values became confused and divided enough to allow an elite of wealthy to take over. We cannot long survive this political polarization in America if we do not find a rallying plan that holds hope and gives sustenance to all of our citizens. We have tried liberal democracy that fell short in the majority's eyes and we are now trying a radical neo-conservative democracy that also seems doomed to failure. Now we are headed back to liberal democracy after the midterm election. Why do not we just try genuine democracy?

Like ours, Roman and Athenian democracy was mostly a club for the rich and did not represent small people with equality. The seeds of discontent and disaffection of the common people was feared, however. The discontent was assuaged by theater, games and a dole much as it is today. There isn't a lot of difference between gladiators and football players except for the degree of lethality. Every sizable Roman city had a large arena where gladiators entertained the populace with lethal personal contests to the death. It is mind boggling to think how many people for centuries must have been slaughtered in these contests to win popular support for Roman rule.

We need renovation of our whole system, especially the presidency. Our gamble on voting into power a man we really know little about is a dangerous unnecessary gamble. We better change this roll of the dice before it turns out to be a total disaster such as we may now have. One Caligula or Hitler can undo an empire in no time at all. We need to know more about the man who is to lead us and his plan before we elect him. Then we must give him the legislative power to carry out his plan swiftly and surely. If he lies to us or proves to be incompetent we cannot afford to sit back and write-off four-eight years as we now do. We should have a right, in the form of a regular mandated vote of confidence, to recall him. If the electorate were given such an option, it is unlikely that it would need to be used as often as it does today. With this political Sword of Damocles hanging over his head, it is unlikely the President would be so ready to lie and commit other acts of malfeasance. And it might prevent the repetition of the Supreme Court appointing a president that in my view is a disaster.

Our system, in America, has become finicky and lacks continuity. One year we stand for a great society, a war on poverty, human rights, peace with everybody and the next year we want to stick our heads in the sand and let business go on as usual in the slums of the world, back the most repressive dictatorships and spend every cent we can scrape together on armaments. It makes one seriously consider whether he is living in the same country from one administration to the next. Morally and materially, America has become a land of contradictions. The quality of life for the average person has deteriorated to the point that we hardly recognize America as the same country it was twenty or thirty years ago. Everything is very expensive, especially for those just getting started or on fixed incomes, especially housing, which is through the roof. We certainly have very limited opportunity in America compared to what we used to have. Economically, most of the opportunity has moved overseas, because we cannot compete in so many things we used to excel in. Americans are far from the top of the list in per capita income. As bad as it is here, it could get a lot worse, and probably will, before there is any improvement. Many Americans wonder if we do live in the best of existing countries, but not for long if they travel extensively abroad, where, in most places, the problems are similar or worse than ours. This does not make it right here or abroad that the quality of life is deteriorating the way it is.

As does any country, we have a peculiar culture that we are firmly convinced is the best in the world. I share this prejudice and believe our culture to be the neatest and most stimulating in the world. I also think America, in spite of a great deal of antipathy about culture, is in many ways the most culturally evolved country in the world; this is in spite of the punk rockers, sports enthusiast dullards and ubiquitous pornography. Can you imagine how strange we must seem to the belly dance culture? The Dalai Lama has been recently quoted as saying, "seeing American lifestyle represented on T.V. has made these backward cultures jealous and this is the root of their hatred of America". I agree 100 %. Our present culture in America (And Great Britain that has a very similar culture) has evolved out of a tradition of personal freedom mainly made possible by the First Amendment protection of freedom of speech, a tradition that is probably unprecedented in the history of the world.

This personal freedom, however, has not been achieved automatically as a spin-off blessing of the system. Much of it has been won by hard fighting that is little understood inside or outside of America. Since the sixties, and this is what the sixties and seventies were all about, personal freedom in America has been extended almost to another dimension, and this has made a great impression on the rest of the world. There was a mainland Chinese author-filmmaker who got in trouble because he made a film in which the main character, a writer who, after a visit to America, says there is only one country where there is a "shining brightness." This "shining brightness" he was referring to certainly was not our inner city slums. It is brightness of the soul of America represented since the 1960's generation that has revolutionized personal freedom. The rebels without a cause really did have a cause, even though they did not bother to understand it very well. That cause was the beginnings of the revolution of personal freedom that has swept America.

This personal freedom side of America is the facet of America that is its "shining brightness", and the side that everyone, except old fashioned Ayatollah's, love and admire and sometimes mistake for the whole of America. Unfortunately it is not the whole America. It is limited freedom that has often been won by terrible personal sacrifice. And to some degree, the masters of greed to mask their own rapacious takeover of the American political system use it.

Some of the manifestations of this personal freedom revolution are: sexual liberation, the abolition of censorship that has in turn made a revolution in theater, music and the other arts possible, the feminist movement, abortion rights, and, to some degree, civil rights (The civil rights and the personal freedom movements have fed on each other, but each really happened independently), and last but by no means least, a personal right to choose whether one should fight for one's country by coercion or voluntarily. So far, the concept of an all-volunteer military has been working well, but the sick stupidly bungled war we were lied into in Iraq is threatening to undermine this step forward. When every human being has a democratic right to say no to participating in war, we will not so readily attempt to solve our problems by war. "One's country right or wrong" should be "one's country, only if I believe it is right", except in dire emergency. No one should be forced to fight in a war he does not believe in. All this personal freedom has not been won without some martyrs. The war is still going on and, as in any war; a war is not won by winning a few easy victories. Apparently, Bush didn't know this when he declared the Iraq war over. There are repressive reactionary forces, which, reeling for the moment, have regrouped themselves under various newspeak names and are more organized and better financed than any time in our history. We of opposing beliefs must organize to meet this threat, or we are going to be swallowed by a killer whale of reactionary despots waiting in the depths. They will indeed turn the clock back if we let them.

We must all come to terms with what we are or we will be divided and conquered culturally, as we have been politically and economically. We the people who are participating in the personal freedom revolution are, quite frankly, fun loving, freedom loving, culture freaks that do not want any part of the homogenization and robotization of man. We want to do our own thing without outside interference or being a party to the greedy exploitation of

our fellow man. We believe in brotherly and sisterly love, sharing and prosperity for every person. We want to grow and fulfill ourselves in our own way and we want everyman to have the same opportunity. America, and we should have no delusions about it, is hated by much of the oppressed majority of the world. We are hated as well by jealous rivals for the hearts and minds of humanity. It is we, the culture freaks, who, in spite of all manner of repression short of an actual police state, have overcome the tarnished superficial shine of America and made this country glitter in the imagination of the people of the world. The people of the world should not mistake our face as the whole face of America. There is another face. The crass materialism face associated with previous generations. We are the bright shining soul of America. However, the mainstream establishment will, as it has done to some degree already, preempt us and take credit for our victories, if we let them. And then they will bastardize our culture and repackage us to make us profitable to them like Total, the breakfast cereal, loaded with MDR vitamins of questionable value that claims to out-natural natural, a pack of oxymoron lies. What it really does is put the bucks back in the coffers of big business. The masters of greed do not give up easy. If they cannot get us to buy their adulterated white Wonder bread glue one way, they trick us, and. get away with it because we have a no-account, useless, incompetent big business controlled government that is too small and weak to enforce the law if it exists at all. Put that in your government is too big pipe and smoke it, you sophist liars. The theology of the business establishment in the United States is very similar to that which the Moonies Unification Church preaches to the suckers that fall for it. And there have been many. They loudly proclaim in their dogma, "all money that does not belong to Reverend Moon belongs to Satan". Moon's followers have a practice called "divine deception" that is their method of tricking unsuspecting people into buying their products. I wonder if they apply this to their newspaper editorials in the scurrilously right wing Washington Times. Unless the Moonies own all the bread companies in America, Madison Avenue knew their method of divine deception long before Moon. The staff of life has been converted into the staff of death, poisoning Americans with adulterated pseudo food and cancer causing chemicals every time we put this wonder food glue into our mouths. All the deceptively dishonest Moonie subversion they are so proud of is currently financed by their virtual monopoly on Sushi supplied to restaurants under the umbrella of a non-*prophet* corporation (*joke*) that makes big profits for their self-proclaimed prophet Moon. I boycott Sushi. So should you unless you like parasites.

Culture huggers are those spectators or participants in culture who will not tolerate any censorship of lifestyle or personal freedom. They are the representatives of the peaceful Cultural Revolution that has taken place in America since the 1960's. It is the cultural freedom revolution that is the America that most people think of when they think of American freedom. The personal freedom revolution began as a freedom of speech revolution. The First Amendment to the Constitution, which includes freedom of speech and assembly, is what has made possible the revolution of culture we have lived through. It is the impetus for everything and must be protected at all costs.

Hopefully the personal freedom revolution will be known as the peaceful revolution. It must continue because it is and must be the foundation on which true democracy can be built. John Lennon was a leading voice for the personal freedom revolution and may well have been its first casualty. The man who murdered him was a former Neo Nazi. I once marched in a small protest parade in London with John and Yoko and about three hundred other protestors against the obscenity bust of Oz magazine, one of the finest examples of the then flourishing underground press syndicate. Talk about establishment overkill. There were about three hundred of us followed by about three hundred cops. When we got to the place where the American embassy was located, which had, nothing to do with the protest, this seeming mile long building was completely surrounded by Bobbies, linked elbows to asswholes. Talk about establishment overkill. We rambled all over London shouting surrealistic obscenities like "down with fried eggs". Every once in a while we would stop for a rest in the middle of some busy thoroughfare and after a short time the police would give us an ultimatum to move or be busted. Someone would ask for a vote by acclamation whether to move on or be busted. We always voted to move on until after many hours we arrived back at the same place we started, Marble Arch in the park. We had a great time protesting for a very just cause and creating a little fear in a very paranoid establishment. I was just one of the little faceless people in that crowd of three hundred, but it was fine to march with John and

Yoko because they were not anybody special that day. They took the same risk the rest of us took for the same pay; a reassertion of our free personhood.

I had gone to London to try and rally support for another group on the leading edge of the Cultural Revolution, The Living Theater. The whole group was in jail in Brazil in dire straights and as I subsequently learned when they got back home, being tortured. They fortunately didn't suffer any permanent damage to their lives, but they were lucky. This was a severe right wing dictatorship era in Brazil when many of the locals weren't so lucky.

Another leading edge personality of the personal freedom revolution who became a martyr was Abbie Hoffman. I had asked him to star in a play called Che! that I directed in the late sixties, but he declined due to ill health at the time. The Che! play was subsequently busted for 52 counts of obscenity that resulted in a landmark trial that was finally won on appeal with the help of the ACLU. This was no thanks to the many police who lied under oath at the trial. This broke me financially, but also broke the back of censorship in New York theater at the same time. Henceforth, N.Y.C. theatrical companies did not have to sweat the censorship problem that had plagued us previously. Lucky for Abbie, he declined to do the play, as he was still recovering from a severe illness or he would have been in double trouble when he got busted as one of the Chicago seven principals. After that I did not see him for many years until he was appearing at a nightclub in Los Angeles called the Palomino about six months before his death by suicide. I was standing in a dark ticket line waiting to go into the nightclub when he came walking by and to my great surprise, he some how spotted and recognized me and said, Hi Ed as he walked by into the club. His message to the audience was more straight political diatribe, than a comedy act, as I supposed it was going to be, and centered on the idea of America becoming a mixed economy. Not very politically revolutionary or funny at the time, I thought disappointed and it pained me to pretend I was enthusiastic about these ideas, I thought to be what America was already about. But he was ahead of his time as usual, already evolving toward the kind of economic and political syntheses I believe I am talking about in these pages. I greatly regret that my own ideas had not evolved to what they are today, so that I might have been more able to be supportive of his views and the friend he may have needed to keep him from the sad

end he came to. I have thought about this many times with deep
sorrow.

Bloody revolutions are crude, unnecessary and as outdated as
duck tails and blue suede shoes. They always seem to end badly. If
one sings, speaks, freaks and loves the truth, all barriers of hate and
greed can be overcome. The majority of the members of the human
race, especially the young, are truth seeking and will get in line to
help create a better world if only given a decent chance. Man can
never solve any problem by shooting his fellow man in the back. The
audacious solidarity of the Mexicans in their recent demonstrations
around the United States proves that non-violent protest is very
effective, as it was in the civil rights movement. There is safety in
numbers. The Mexicans and the Wildebeests prove that.

We must continue to try freeing man so that he can choose his own
style of life or death. Choice is what life is all about. Parity stands for
a society that is rich enough for man to fully develop his highest and
most spiritual aspirations. This means complete personal freedom to
make life-fulfilling choices. I think the old Confucian concept of the
golden mean, or moderation in all things, is preferable to any extreme,

although there are exceptions to everything in life. Man cannot stray very far from nature's rules without paying a heavy penalty.

If there is a universal purpose to life, it is love. Today we do not have any society that can be characterized as a loving society. Parity's ultimate mission is to help instill in man and woman a sense of brotherhood. We have the opposite today, and the result is a murderously dangerous society in which no one anywhere is safe from predators of every imaginable stripe, running the gamut from street muggers to white collar swindlers and lying talk radio hosts, maybe the worst of all, as they rob people of the truth.

We should begin to build a pyramid of love that will put the humpty dumpy of divided, disenfranchised man back together again. We need to reorder our priorities, a much used and much abused term. We need to turn this and other hot air rhetoric from empty posturing to hardheaded, pragmatic action. Most simply put, we have to become a problem-solving society, as opposed to a problem society. We must find practical solutions for problems. Practice is the best crucible for solving problems. We have to become a humane democratic society that has no doubt about whether butter is a better choice than guns. A society that is chronically dependent on the military-industrial complex for prosperity and dominance is a death-oriented society. We must choose between building a world forever dependent on the economic dole or a world based on developing in every country a healthy industry based on a Parity equality of fair competition. This is the choice between a death or a life civilization. We must choose between a society based on a bottom line of prosperity and equality or a society of hateful conflict between "haves" and "have nots." We must choose between a weak, ineffectual government dependent on a self-interest oriented business community or a strong effective central government representing the broad interests of the whole organic society. We need to choose whether the agency of government or business is capable of attacking national problems such as housing, energy, underemployment, interest rates, global warming etc. Then we must decide whether we are going to form a plan to attack these problems or stick our heads in a dung heap and hope for a miracle, as we are now doing. These and other choices have to be made. It is really a choice between the pseudo democracy we now have or genuine democracy.

Most big businesses that are going under in the West are reemerging in Asia, where economic factors make them once again viable business enterprises. That we are allowing this to happen in every Western country is plumb dumb clueless leadership. Out of balance economic factors should not be allowed to dictate whether industries will flourish or go under and take our jobs with them. What is the point of world free trade if it destroys the economy of a country in the process? It is time to change the world economic order from a game of musical chairs that has a few winners and a lot of losers to one in which every country is a winner. The entire world manufacturing economy cannot gravitate to China, as it is trending, at the expense of the rest of the world. If this is the definition of globalization, it is a disaster.

In its simplest form Parity could be described as an organic society in which all aspects of society have an obligation to cooperate with all other aspects of society in creating prosperity. By cooperation, we do not mean subject to coercion. There are many pitfalls that either inadvertently or intentionally prevent what by all rights should be an organic democratic society in America. They are the divide and conquer techniques. But in modern times, the people of America have been easily divided and conquered by politicians who do not really represent their interests. In the United States the establishment has a way of perceiving any major threat to its power structure and reacting by buying off enough pressure on the threatened part to protect the whole system of inequality.

The major labor unions were once just such a threat. In recent times these unions have succeeded in bringing enough pressure to bare on employers that their members are among the best paid workers in the world. Various stratagems are being used to take away the political power from unions. Govenator Schwarzenegger (Special election Ca 2005) of California tried to pass an initiative that would have emasculated unions in California, but it failed at the ballot box. If it had passed, unions would not have been able to make campaign contributions that they consider to be in their best interest. Hopefully it had the opposite effect intended, but shameless chameleon that he is; he is now trying to pass himself off as a centrist populist similar to a California Democrat. Because it is an election year, he has recently restored cuts he made to education and other beneficial programs that affect the poor and old.

Workers in weak or corrupt unions, on the other hand, have little or no say and get low pay. And what is worse, workers in non-union industries are usually not paid anything close to the wages paid in major unionized industries. The minimum wage in America is certainly not enough to escape poverty, and most people will not work for it if they can otherwise help themselves. What logical reason could there be for paying workers in some industries that are unionized many times what workers in another non- union industry get. The answer is that there is no logic to it or to our entire economic system anymore. Of course, McDonald's is taking advantage of these divided and conquered workers to make a lot of money that should be going to workers. McDonald's employees work the same amount of hours as workers in other industries, so why should they not receive comparable compensation for their time? They should be of course. The answer as to why they are not, the only true answer, is that such non-union workers have no voice, because organized labor has limited its scope on most unskilled workers and allowed them to thus be divided and conquered. On the other hand, McDonald's, which has a huge concentration of capital to use for political purposes, applies lobbying pressure to keep the minimum wage standard of living low.

The labor unions in the major industries have succeeded in obtaining a fair and sometimes what seems like an excessive wage for their workers, but the question is, at what price? These same labor unions have never exercised their economic muscle to have a say in the operation of the companies their members work for and are invested in through their pension funds. Of course, under laws favorable to companies, they couldn't, because the companies, not the union workers, legally control the worker pension funds. This is one of the legal peculiarities that American capitalism has been able to put into place to stack the deck in its favor. The union people who let them get away with this must have been either retards or corrupt or just plain stupid. If workers did have some control of the company, I am sure worker productivity and cooperation would be better. Of course this is getting to be a moot point, as it appears pensions are on the way out, to be replaced by 401Ks. In this vein of what really makes workers happy, The Los Angeles Times, made its own survey of workers across the United States: the survey revealed that American workers expect more from their jobs than just money. #1 is having an interesting job. #2 is having a job that gives them a sense of accomplishment. #3 is a job that gives them prestige. And in forth place is money. Workers are not, contrary to popular belief, money hungry animals intent only on gouging as much money as they can from their employers.

A second way the unions have copped-out is by ignoring the destruction of the economy as discussed above. Certainly, if my job were being exported because my industry can produce more cheaply abroad or if my job were being lost to unfair competition from abroad, I would have a lot more to say about how the companies I work for and own a large interest in through my pension fund was being operated. Of course, unfair undemocratic laws usually prevent this input. The major labor union movement in the United States crested a long time ago and has for reasons of self interest apparently decided to play it safe with the established worker unions and not rock the boat. Like the mythical Atlantians, the major union's boat will be on the bottom of the sea before they wake up and realize it is sinking fast. And so will we if global warming isn't stopped. There is a new movement to unionize professionals and tech workers that is meeting with some success. Hopefully this will succeed before all their jobs get outsourced.

The third copout criticism of the unions is that they have ignored the plight of the broad mass of workers in the United States who are low end. I think the rational for ignoring fellow workers is that the less these workers get, the more workers that are unionized can get.

There is no doubt that the unions have inadvertently or otherwise joined the establishment to rip-off the divided and conquered non-union workers of America. I suppose these other workers are the great American individualists we are always hearing about. This is another of the myths that divide and conquer. The concept of the individualist being chiefly responsible for America's greatness is an anachronistic pile of pseudo economic bull. It ignores all the people who work for a team. The people in America who work for corporations are the best-paid portion of the work force. The power of these corporations is the backbone of the American economy. Can we suppose the so-called individualist is the corporate executive who usually spent long years working his way up through the corporate bureaucracy of these mini-socialist empires? I don't think so. He may have had to be a selfish backstabber to get to the top, but is this individualism? No way! He is really a team playing bureaucrat who is a part of a team effort; a team effort that plans and executes an economic program that with a great deal of accuracy could be called socialism for the corporate denizens. He, the epitome of modern capitalism, is in no way an individualist. Ergo, people who work for corporations must be communists because they are not individualists. Nothing could be further from the truth.

This is an example, if you try to put the hyped image of the American system one gets in the media together into a consistent logical structure, of just how preposterously contradictory that image is. No wonder people in the United States are so confused.

I cannot resist one more crack at unions. Many unions, like the actor's union (S.A.G.) are no better than extortion rackets as far as I am concerned. Instead of encouraging membership these unions do everything in their power to keep others out of their union. Even when people do qualify to join this union, there is an exorbitant amount charged the usually starving actor to join the union. I think all workers in this country should have a union voice and be able to join unions without being charged any money up front to join. After joining and earning some money, they will be able to afford to pay an initiation fee and pay dues. Hollywood unions should learn that the horse and not the other way around pulls a chariot. Certainly Hollywood, which has always put untrained and untried "actors" in front of cameras, is no place to start claiming someone has to learn his craft before qualifying for a job. That is all bunk designed to reduce job competition.

Another aspect of the L.A. Times survey entitled "Basic Work Ethic Found to Endure", is that 70% of workers surveyed said they would rather work than be paid not to work for the rest of their lives. Another insidious technique for slandering the common man in America and dividing public opinion is to say that he has gotten lazy and does not want to work anymore. This leads into a really beguiling line of reasoning, which concludes that because he will not work at substandard wages the American worker has gotten lazy. Anyone who has seen the conditions that illegal alien migrant Mexicans live in to hold these substandard jobs realizes how the purveyors of these jobs would like to see the whole human race, except themselves, live, like animals.

Call it brainwashing or whatever lesser degree of sin you wish, but there are an insidious number of lies being told, which slander the working man, whitewash what are the real problems, and are lulling us all into what is going to end in the greatest economic and political catastrophe the world has ever seen, if we do not get busy and turn over a new leaf.

There are other forms of divide and conquer techniques being used, including the old states rights trick. That term is not heard as frequently these days since the Republicans have come to power. It seems that when there is no other way to destroy a proposed piece of national legislation, a sure fire method is claim states rights status for it and shift it to the individual states, which have even more corrupt and ineffective legislative systems than the federal government could ever dream of. The federal government is no slouch itself though. I saw a program once on Sixty Minutes about how it is determined which cities and counties should receive distressed cities status, and thus qualify for distress funds from the federal government. A computer figured all this out, the most recent data of which was ten years old or older. Consequently, Orange County, Florida, one of the richest, least distressed counties in the country, was considered qualified for distress funds and applied for them. If they're still using the same computer, New Orleans will probably never be rebuilt. They'll rebuild San Francisco before it needs it instead, just in time for the next apocalyptic earthquake. This is an utter outrage to see our tax dollars so misused and is certainly fuel for the propaganda mill of those who oppose government. What really blows me away are the many shocking exposes you see on 60 minutes and some other programs and none of it much seems to make a dent in the psyche of the nation. It hardly makes a ripple Helen.

We still contend that the federal government is suffering from a morale problem, because it is the engrained philosophy of many of those charged with its functioning, especially political spoils appointees, to not believe in its efficacy. Many of the political appointee executive heads of agencies are charged with duties they are not expert at from previous jobs. If hiring incompetent people would be a moronic monstrosity in private industry, why is it allowed in government? One reason is that government is considered by the Republicans to be a worthless nuisance at best. The point of bureaucracy, whether in private industry or government, is supposed to be checks and balances against rampant incompetence. However, private industry is supposed to work, government is not. And when it doesn't, it reinforces the philosophy of the Republicans that government cannot do anything right. We certainly recommend some better system of accountability in the government than now exists, including making the firing of incompetent civil service workers easier. And the heads of most departments are still political appointees, as was FEMA head Brown who was in charge during

Katrina. We really never got totally rid of the spoils system, but we should. This obliterates another pseudo icon of our pseudo democracy.

Just plain political rhetoric turns an easy divide and conquer trick. Rhetoric is a name for one of the world's first euphemisms meaning trick speaking (Get this pun! Rhe-trick). The politicians consider an election to be like Halloween. Trick the public and they'll treat you fine. And the anchor pseudo press let's them get away with it because it is populated by uninformed hacks. Any sign of intelligence in this group is as scarce as a Faberge egg at an Easter egg hunt. It seems obvious that news anchors are picked for being dumb and uninformed so that the news can be manipulated without any static from the hired hands. Their main qualification is to be able to read a teleprompter, look, and sound good. When they open their mouths to comment or ask a question, the result is appalling. The American public had better start studying more closely the men and women who are running for office, or we are going to make the kind of mistake that has been made before. Adolph Hitler was elected to office democratically. Maybe they should break the news to George W. Bush.

The purpose of this book is not to point out every abuse of the democratic system or we would have to write an encyclopedia of abuses, which might not be a bad idea for some political science student's thesis project. We are just trying to say enough to illustrate how far America has gone down the road to democratic despotism; and how we can hopefully reform an obsolete system and reunite the American people, who for the most part, are a generous, loving, hard working people deserving a better informed, united democracy that does not prey on natural human gullibility. No one is going to help us if we do not help ourselves.

There is every reason to believe that we are in mortal danger of economic and political disaster. For the first time since World War II we are faced with foreign competition that is clearly eroding the economic strength of our country. And the situation is not likely, for reasons pointed out above, to get any better. I once read an article in the L.A. Times entitled "New Businesses Help to Change China's Life". This article left little doubt that the Chinese were forming a new economy based on part capitalism and part socialism. This time, it seems, the grafting of capitalism to socialism is going to be a permanent feature of the Chinese system. The new mixed capitalist-socialist approach to solving economic problems is turning China from a third world country to an economic powerhouse. This new paradigm will continue to succeed as long as the rest of the world cooperates. The way things are going China may soon be the sole occupant of the economic musical chairs.

Economics, like love, seems to thrive on strange bedfellows. The central government of China is in partnership with the American Coca Cola Company. We may well be seeing the emergence of the next evolutionary generation of economic-political systems. The central government in China is functioning much like the biblical kingdom of Egypt which, because of a warning from Joseph, a Hebrew counselor to the Egyptian pharaoh, stored grain for famine years, except China is not only storing grain but also is storing lots of money and other things. China, for the first time in its long history, has prepared itself adequately to cope with various emergencies that otherwise had dire consequences in the past. Because of infrastructure improvements, such as huge damns on rivers that used to flood and other infrastructure improvements the central government is able to provide a safety net for over one billion people who otherwise might fall victim of flood and famine, their historical nemeses.

Presently the Chinese government is pragmatically experimenting with the concept of a mixed capitalist-socialist economy. I think this step is now a fully integrated part of their communist system, but unfortunately it has become entrenched capitalism of the most exploitative kind. This combination of the best of both economic worlds could well make China what it intends to become; the

greatest economic powerhouse in the world. The Chinese fully intend making the Asian tiger economic miracle their own economic dragon. In fact, Japan's economic miracle that had been in the doldrums for years is once more taking on life, because it has a new huge market in China for investment and products. Technology and capital are more readily available to the Chinese with each passing day and they are fast becoming the consumer goods engine of the whole world.

We are calling on all Americans to wake up and take a more pragmatic approach to solving our problems. We have the most advanced cultural and technological base in the world today. We are not, however, long going to enjoy this lead, if we do not become a super capitalism that can compete on a fair basis with other countries. Societies, like people, must grow or become dwarfs. It has happened to innumerable societies in the history of the world, including the

Chinese in all but the size of their population. It will happen to America if we continue to allow ourselves to be ruled by incompetents and by a system long overdue for bottom-to-top renovation. I believe it was Benjamin Franklin and or Jefferson who said that it is every man's duty to overthrow a tyrant. The tyrant in this case is we the people, truly. We just refuse to wake up and solve our problems. And now we are taking the dangerous step of allowing ourselves to be bought and sold by those who are little better than white-collar crooks. People who have no respect for the personal rights we have fought so hard for in the last decades, are able, with the financial backing of corporations to hound from office, in the name of the Almighty, the politicians who have most attempted to speak for the interests of the people. They are our only hope until we get off our doffs and give them some help by reforming this muscle-bound system.

I think America today is best summed up by the Mormen woman whose husband, John Singer, was murdered, as far as I am concerned, by the authorities because he choose not to send his children to schools that did not teach values he could agree with or condone. I do not endorse his values by any stretch of the imagination, but certainly

I loudly protest that he had a right to choose his own lifestyle without being murdered by the government. His wife, who is carrying on his struggle for personal freedom, is quoted as saying, "I am caretaker over these, my children, that the Lord has given unto my hands. The state did not bear my children, I did. The state didn't cloth and feed my children. My husband did." And she might have added in all truth; "and God knows, we have a President and government who are not going to do anything for anybody but rich people, if it can help it. So why should I send my children to your schools and have their heads filled with ideas that will make my children ready dupes of a system that has lost any semblance of a moral compass?"

I recently watched an episode of Foreign Exchange with Fareed Zakaria on PBS that included a segment of the show about the attempt of Ghana to establish a local textile/clothing manufacturing industry. It illustrated better than all the words in this book why a Parity economic system is needed. They have been trying to establish a textile/ready-wear manufacturing industry based on their own indigenous designs and textiles. The Chinese came in with low priced ready-wear and under cut them. What they have done to survive is to turn one day a week into what they call, "Casual Friday Wear" or

"National Friday Wear day". People that can afford it, wear the beautiful locally hand made and designed clothes. But their ready-wear industry cannot compete with the Chinese. My question to the world is, where is the global conscience for this globalization that precludes nations such as Ghana from developing an economic system that provides needed local jobs. The answer is simple; this global free market system (So-called) that already has concentrated half the world's manufactories in China is unconscionably turning the rest of the world into failed states. Is this not the source cause of most of the illegal immigration that is headed to America and Europe? Who is going to stay in a country that has no jobs and no hope of creating them? This issue has to be addressed or the present immigration situation is going to turn into a Tsunami. Globalization in its present form is a disaster for countries such as Ghana. And in the long run it is going to be a disaster for everybody as some countries with all the jobs fill up to the bursting point with immigrants and other countries that have nothing to sustain their population growth empty out. Or worse, fail completely and become havens for terrorists.

There is much greater alienation in America than is usually perceived to be the case. The reason only half the people vote is that at least half are convinced, along with Gore Vidal, one of our most brilliant writers, that to vote is a waste of time. To vote, except in a negative sense, for the choices we now have is a waste of time. We must have a new choice, a choice that really represents the people and only the people, because now we only have a choice that represents everybody but the people. This choice should have a real ideological rallying point with a difference. One that possesses the will and determination to solve America's vast problems and reaffirm us as a healthy viable economic powerhouse second to none. Parity Equality is one such hypothetical possibility.

I make no claim to have all the answers. That we do need a new people-centered party and political movement is a certainty. No system should ever become as dogmatic as ours has become. No one is taken seriously that thinks our political-economic system is obsolete and needs vast changes. That is intellectually lazy uninformed blindness to reality. That is what is wrong with the world now. Systems, like people, sometimes develop arteriosclerosis and need literal rotorooting renewal. If we have not made any other point, I hope we have made this one. There is always room for improvement in this world. Parity clearly, loudly, and unequivocally stands for every American being guaranteed, health care, a decent job and real education. Only when these things are part of the constitution will we have real democracy. Only then should we call ourselves a democracy. People must have an interesting job and good wages that will support a family. This family should be able to live in such a way that all its members have an opportunity to fulfill their lives by becoming suitably educated. Corporate dictatorship is never going to give us these things. Only real democracy can. Down with the minimum wage! Up with the maximum wage!

FINI

www.ingramcontent.com/pod-product-compliance
Lightning Source LLC
Chambersburg PA
CBHW031503270326
41930CB00006B/220